Trotsky

FOR BEGINNERS

Tariq Ali   & Phil Evans

Writers and Readers

First published 1980 by
Writers and Readers Publishing Cooperative Limited,
9-19 Rupert Street, London, W1V 7FS, England

Text copyright © 1980 **Tariq Ali**
Illustrations © 1980 **Phil Evans**

Series editor **Richard Appignanesi**
Documentary photos courtesy **David King**
Cover design by **Louise Fili**
Corrections by **Jill Wallis**
Typesetting **Feb Edge Litho**, London
Printed and bound in the United States of America

Typeset by **Linda Quinn** in 14/18pt Times and 12pt Univers
Line prints and halftones processed at **Feb Edge Litho**

Case **ISBN** o 906495 27 X
Paper **ISBN** 0 906495 28 8

Trotsky for Beginners

Trotsky was the revolutionary closest to Lenin. Lenin called him "the ablest man in the Party . . ."

MARX   ENGELS   LENIN   STALIN

But it was Stalin, not Trotsky, who rose to power after Lenin's death. Stalin tried everything to make Trotsky disappear from 'official' Soviet history. Censorship removed Trotsky from all pictures which showed him as a leader of the Russian Revolution next in importance to Lenin.

Made of metal, nickel-plated.

Trotsky became a "non-person" . . .

For Stalin and his orthodox Communist followers, Trotsky became the devil incarnate. Every disaster at home, every set-back abroad could be explained away by blaming the "Trotskyite-fascist-wreckers". In Moscow and Peking today the Trotskyite "criminal heresy" is still regarded as the worst sin of all.

In 1956, at the 20th Party Congress, when Krushchev denounced the "crimes of Stalin", what did Mao call him?

In 1960, when the Chinese split with the Russians and accused them of putting "peaceful co-existence" before revolution, what did Krushchev call Mao?

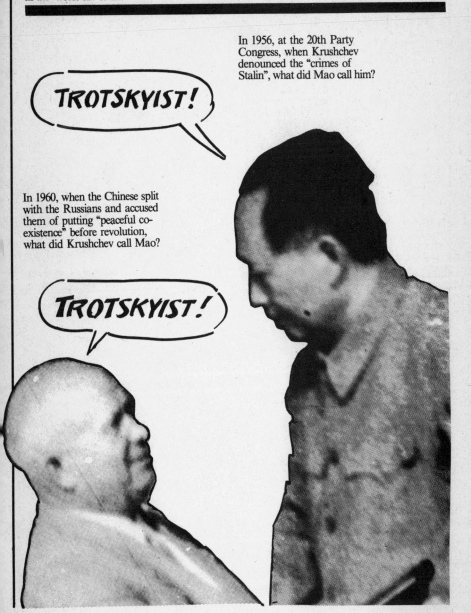

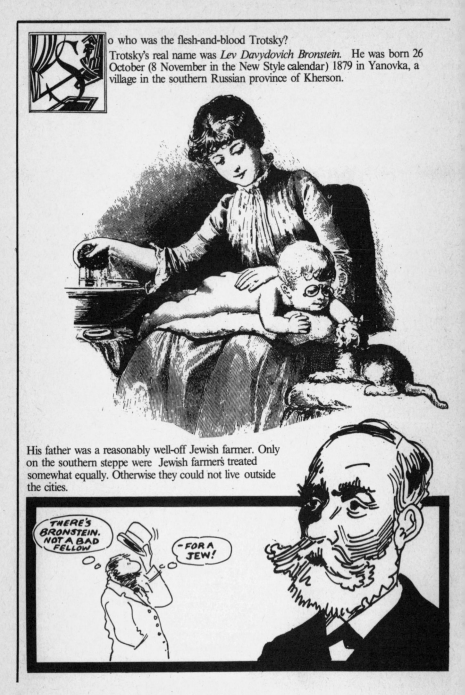

o who was the flesh-and-blood Trotsky?

Trotsky's real name was *Lev Davydovich Bronstein.* He was born 26 October (8 November in the New Style calendar) 1879 in Yanovka, a village in the southern Russian province of Kherson.

His father was a reasonably well-off Jewish farmer. Only on the southern steppe were Jewish farmers treated somewhat equally. Otherwise they could not live outside the cities.

THERE'S BRONSTEIN. NOT A BAD FELLOW

—FOR A JEW!

The year of Trotsky's birth saw the Narodnik* movement begin its offensive against the Tsarist autocracy. Narodniks believed that Russia could bypass Western capitalism by creating a socialism based on peasant revolution. Their language was dynamite!

Alexander II

In March 1881 Narodnik activists killed the Tsar. But they also committed suicide as an organisation. Repression was severe.

*THERE IS A WHOS WHO AT THE BACK OF THIS BOOK

At the age of ten Trotsky was packed off to study in Odessa.
Here he discovered books and Italian opera.

"*For several months I was mutely
in love with the coloratura
soprano . . . who seemed to me to
have descended straight from
heaven to the stage boards of
Odessa.*"

"*A well-written book in which
one can find new ideas, and a
good pen with which to
communicate one's own ideas to
others, for me have always been
and are today the most valuable
and intimate products of
culture.*" **from** *My Life, Trotsky*

In summer, the teen-aged Trotsky, now well-dressed and wearing glasses, would return to his father's farm —where he looked, and felt, out of place. He got "all excited and used harsh words" because the peasants did not accept that geometry was a quicker and better method to measure a trapezoidal field.

YOU'RE **STUPID!** WHY DON'T YOU USE MY **SCIENTIFIC METHOD?**

BECAUSE, WHEN WE'VE MEASURED THE FIELD **ACCURATELY** WITH OUR WOODEN TRIANGLE, AND COMPARE OUR RESULT WITH YOURS—

— YOURS IS ALWAYS **WRONG!**

Trotsky was always quick-tempered, arrogant and a stubborn believer in intellectual solutions.

Trotsky's studies next took him to Nikolaev, a small sea-port town. Here, in 1896 he attends a socialist discussion circle which met in an orchard. Alexandra Sokolovskaya, a Marxist, was invited to the circle. She argued in favor of proletarian socialism against all varieties of Narodnik peasant socialism. Trotsky defended the Narodniks.

Alexandra Sokolovskaya (standing) with (left to right) her brother Ilya, G.A. Ziv, and Trotsky, aged eighteen.

At the Nikolaev circle's New Year's Eve party in 1896 Trotsky proposes a toast to tease Alexandra.

A curse on all Marxists, and upon those who want to bring dryness and hardness into all relations of life!

LEV DAVYDOVICH, SOME THINGS ARE TOO SACRED TO JOKE ABOUT!

Alexandra Sokolovskaya won the debate in the end.

13

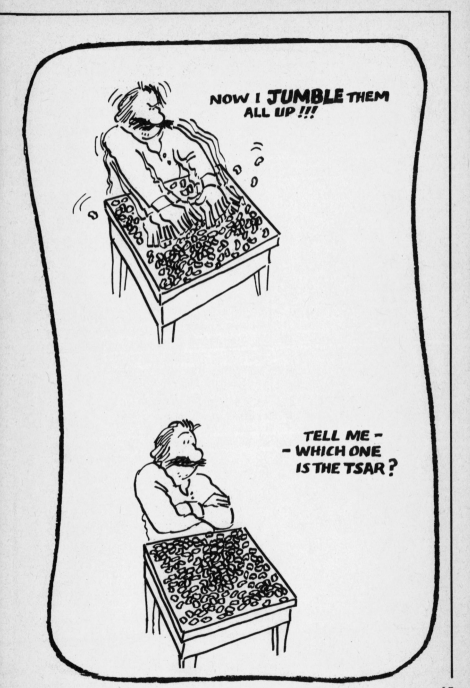

15

With Alexandra's brother, Gregory, and other friends, Trotsky begins clandestine activity and organises the South Russian Workers Union in 1897. The Tsarist police quickly hit back in 1898. Trotsky was arrested and placed in solitary confinement. "There were times when I was sick with loneliness . . ."
To while away the time he composed revolutionary limericks. They were never published.

A LIMERICK

RASPUTIN, THE TSARINA'S PRIEST,
WAS COMMONLY KNOWN AS "THE BEAST",
BUT THE COURT DIDN'T CARE
FOR HIS HIPPY-LENGTH HAIR —
HE WAS SHOT, STABBED, AND DROWNED, AT A FEAST.

In a two-year spell in prison Trotsky read Voltaire, Kant and especially Darwin. "Darwin's description of the way in which the pattern on the peacock's feathers formed itself naturally, banished forever the idea of the Supreme Being from my mind."

Charles Darwin

But Darwin himself was not an atheist.

"To the end of my life I shall wonder whether Darwin was sincere in this or whether he merely paid his tribute to conventional beliefs."

from *The Prophet Armed,* **Isaac Deutscher**

17

Trotsky is sentenced to four years deportation in Siberia. In prison he marries his old sparring partner, Alexandra Sokolovskaya, who will accompany him to Siberia.

In the arctic wastelands, 1902, Trotsky receives Lenin's book, *What Is To Be Done?* and some copies of the revolutionary newspaper *Iskra*.

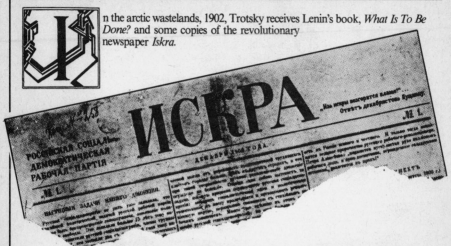

In *What Is To Be Done?* Lenin argues against all notions of workers being spontaneously capable of overthrowing their oppressors. Workers may develop trade unions; but that won't automatically make them political revolutionaries.

Trotsky's writings on politics, art and science appear under the name Antid Oto (*antidote* in Italian). His fame as a writer will earn him the nickname Pero, 'the Pen'. But he is impatient in Siberia. In 1902 he says farewell to Alexandra and their two daughters born in Siberia—and escapes.

DON'T GET INTO ANY TROUBLE, DEAR!

He needs a false name in case he's caught and questioned. He chooses the first one that enters his head: *Trotsky*, the name of a warder in Odessa prison.

On an October dawn in 1902 Trotsky knocks at the door of 30 Holford Square, near Kings Cross Station in North London. Inside Lenin and his companion Krupskaya are awakened.

The 'Pen' has arrived!

Krupskaya has to pay for the cab.

Trotsky immediately reports to Lenin on developments in Russia.

In the coming days Lenin shows Trotsky the sights of London—and the possessions of the English ruling class.

But their minds remain on Russia.

Trotsky's talents are obvious. Lenin proposes he joins the *Iskra* editorial board. But one of the veterans on the *Iskra* board, G. V. Plekhanov, known as "the father of Russian Marxism", blocks Trotsky's nomination.

G.V. Plekhanov

For the revolutionary veterans, like Plekhanov, Vera Zasulich, Martov, but especially Lenin, *Iskra* is more than a paper. It is the organisational nucleus of the Russian Social-Democratic Labour Party.

Lenin sends Trotsky on a lecture tour of the Russian colonies in Europe to raise money for *Iskra*. Trotsky's enthusiastic guide around Paris is a Russian student, Natalia Ivanovna Sedova. Though Trotsky was legally married to Alexandra Sokolovskaya, Natalia Sedova became "Mrs Trotsky", bore him two sons, and remained with him till his death.

LONDON 1903: THE 2nd CONGRESS OF THE RUSSIAN SOCIAL-DEMOCRATIC LABOUR PARTY

Today, this Congress is remembered for the political wrangles which split the new-born RSDLP into two factions: the *Bolsheviks* (majority-ites) led by Lenin and the *Mensheviks* (minority-ites) led by Martov and others. These factions soon became the two parties of Russian Marxism with opposed views about revolution.

What was the dispute about? It started with the co-editors of *Iskra*, Lenin and Martov, arguing about party organisation . . .

AN UNDERGROUND PARTY WHICH WANTS TO OVERTHROW THE TSARIST STATE MUST BE STRICTLY CENTRALISED!
Lenin

TROTSKY SUPPORTED MARTOV.

OURS ISN'T A PARTY OF PROFESSIONAL REVOLUTIONARIES BUT ONE OPEN TO ANYONE WHO BELIEVES IN ITS PROGRAMME!
Martov

PLEKHANOV SUPPORTED LENIN.

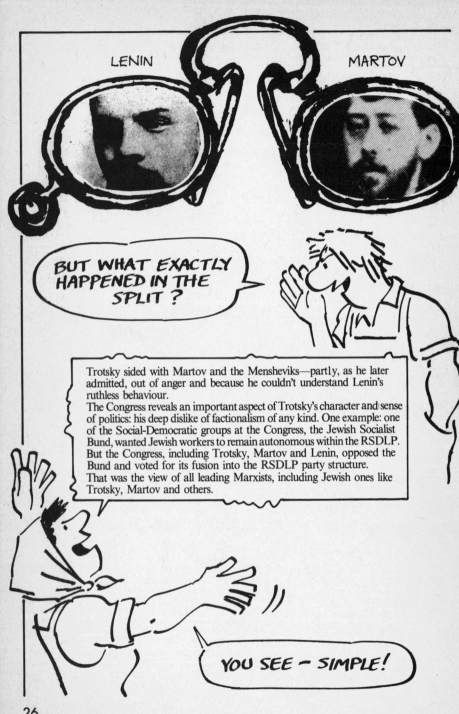

LENIN

MARTOV

BUT WHAT EXACTLY HAPPENED IN THE SPLIT?

Trotsky sided with Martov and the Mensheviks—partly, as he later admitted, out of anger and because he couldn't understand Lenin's ruthless behaviour.

The Congress reveals an important aspect of Trotsky's character and sense of politics: his deep dislike of factionalism of any kind. One example: one of the Social-Democratic groups at the Congress, the Jewish Socialist Bund, wanted Jewish workers to remain autonomous within the RSDLP. But the Congress, including Trotsky, Martov and Lenin, opposed the Bund and voted for its fusion into the RSDLP party structure.

That was the view of all leading Marxists, including Jewish ones like Trotsky, Martov and others.

YOU SEE — SIMPLE!

After the Congress, Plekhanov goes over to the Mensheviks. Lenin withdraws from *Iskra* which is taken over by the Mensheviks. Trotsky, while remaining independent, contributes fiery diatribes against Lenin which the Mensheviks love.
In his battle against Lenin, Trotsky often resorted to vulgar personal abuse.

❝ Marxists, to be sure, especially the Russian ones, were wont to state their views with ruthless frankness. But, as a rule, they refrained from personal mud-slinging. Trotsky's offence against this rule : cannot be explained merely by youthful ebullience – he now exhibited a characteristic of which he could never quite free himself: he could not separate ideas from men. ❞

ISAAC DEUTSCHER

Trotsky remained opposed to Lenin's conception of the party for a whole decade. In *Our Political Tasks* he savagely attacked many of Lenin's formulas:

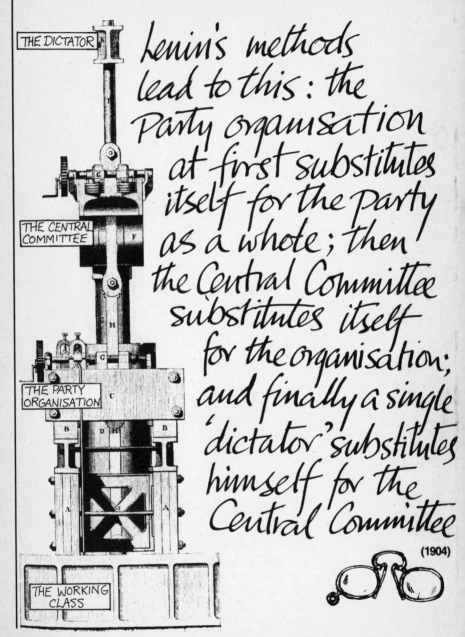

Lenin's methods lead to this: the Party organisation at first substitutes itself for the party as a whole; then the Central Committee substitutes itself for the organisation; and finally a single 'dictator' substitutes himself for the Central Committee

(1904)

Trotsky was later to disown this book. But not completely! He admitted that on the central question of party discipline he had been wrong. But he also insisted that the book contained several insights into the narrow mentality of some Bolshevik committee men of the period. Trotsky was closer to the Menshevik view of the party. But his grasp of revolutionary tactics led him further from them than even Lenin and the Bolsheviks. During every revolutionary upsurge Trotsky was closer to Lenin than many of the Bolshevik committee men.

For many years Trotsky believed a reconciliation between the Mensheviks and Bolsheviks was possible.

1904-1905: THE RUSSO-JAPANESE WAR

This war for colonies in Manchuria, China and Korea ended in defeat for the Tsar's armies. The autocracy was shaken by the experience in the "Manchurian cemetery"; by the rising discontent in the cities and countryside.

Defeat in war—economic and
social crisis—always means a
sharp rise in working-class
consciousness.

A POPULATION OF 150 MILLION PEOPLE, 5.4 MILLION SQUARE KILOMETRES OF LAND IN EUROPE, 17.5 MILLION IN ASIA. WITHIN THIS VAST SPACE EVERY EPOCH OF HUMAN CULTURE IS TO BE FOUND: FROM THE PRIMEVAL BARBARISM OF THE NORTHERN FORESTS, WHERE PEOPLE WORSHIP BLOCKS OF WOOD, TO THE MODERN SOCIAL RELATIONS OF THE CAPITALIST CITY, WHERE SOCIALIST WORKERS CONSCIOUSLY RECOGNISE THEMSELVES AS PARTICIPANTS IN WORLD POLITICS AND KEEP A WATCHFUL EYE ON THE BALKANS AND ON DEBATES IN THE GERMAN REICHSTAG. THE MOST CONCENTRATED INDUSTRY IN EUROPE BASED ON THE MOST BACKWARD AGRICULTURE IN EUROPE. THE MOST COLOSSAL STATE APPARATUS IN THE WORLD MAKING USE OF EVERY ACHIEVEMENT OF MODERN TECHNOLOGICAL PROGRESS IN ORDER TO RETARD THE HISTORICAL PROGRESS OF ITS OWN COUNTRY.

from '1905' TROTSKY.

On the 3rd of January 1905, twelve thousand workers at the Putilov Engineering plants strike.

Troops disperse pickets outside the Putilov works.

31

BLOODY SUNDAY

22 January 1905: 200,000 striking workers in St. Petersburg march to the Winter Palace to petition the Tsar. But the 'Little Father' refuses to see a delegation and orders his troops to disperse the crowds.

TSAR NICHOLAS II

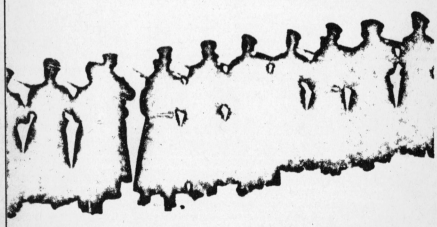

1000 people are shot down.

Within weeks a general strike had developed in towns throughout Russia and a railway strike paralysed the main lines. In a pamphlet written in 1904, submitted to but not published by the Menshevik press, Trotsky had predicted this development with amazing accuracy.

The Tsar offers concessions. The liberal bourgeoisie rush to accept them. How are the liberals organising? Through a political party known as the Constitutional Democrats (referred to by its initials kah-deh as Kadets). Its leader is P. N. Milyukov, an historian. He is rebuked for his capitulation to the Tsar by Trotsky.

Milyukov

If the revolution does not ebb away, the bureaucracy will cling to you as a bulwark; and if you really try to become its bulwark, the victorious revolution will throw you overboard . . . (if, on the other hand, the revolution is defeated, then Tsardom will have no use for liberalism). You propose not to be disturbed by the voices from the right and voices from the left . . . The revolution has not yet said its last word. With powerful and broad thrusts it lowers the edge of its knife over the head of absolutism. Let the wiseacres of liberalism beware of putting their hands under the glittering steel blade. Let them beware . . .

TROTSKY **from** The Prophet Armed, **Isaac Deutscher**

33

The 1905 Revolution was a "general dress-rehearsal". It severely dented the Tsarist autocracy, but could not overthrow it. From that, the Russian proletariat learned many new lessons—and the most important one was the formation of . . .

THE PETERSBURG SOVIET OF WORKERS' DEPUTIES

Trotsky (centre left) with members of the Soviet

The first appearance of democratic power in modern Russian history!
There was real democracy, with the voters' right to recall their deputies at
any moment.

WHAT IS A SOVIET, EXACTLY?

AH - GOOD QUESTION!

SORRY BROTHER. WE ELECTED YOU TO DO WHAT WE WANTED. YOU DIDN'T - SO WE'VE SACKED YOU !!!

The Soviet is an embryo of a revolutionary government. It organises a free press. It organises street patrols to secure the safety of the citizens. It takes over the post office... the railroads... The first wave of the next revolution will lead to the creation of Soviets all over the country.

Trotsky

Petersburg had a half-million-strong proletarian population. Of these, the Soviet represented about half, mostly factory and plant workers.

BUT THE SOVIET REPRESENTS —

— <u>ALL</u> OUR INTERESTS!

Who was against the soviet? The representatives of predatory capitalism...

The Bolsheviks were slow to respond. Only when Lenin returned did they act.

GUILTY - OF INDECISION!

The Soviet only lasted 50 days. On 16 December 1905 government troops closed it down and arrested the leaders. The revolution had been defeated.

Trotsky was 26 years old. His speech in court was an address to the world.

GUILTY - OF BEING TROTSKY!

A rising of the masses is not made, gentlemen the judges. It makes itself of its own accord.

But the judges are not impressed. Trotsky's trial lasts a year and he is sentenced to Siberia for life!

In prison awaiting trial Trotsky had concentrated on two tasks. The first was reading French novels. " . . . I absorbed them with the same physical delight with which the gourmet sips choice wine or inhales the fragrant smoke of a fine cigar . . ." **from** *My Life*, **Trotsky**

Right: Balzac, by Rodin

PERMANENT REVOLUTION

Permanent in what way?

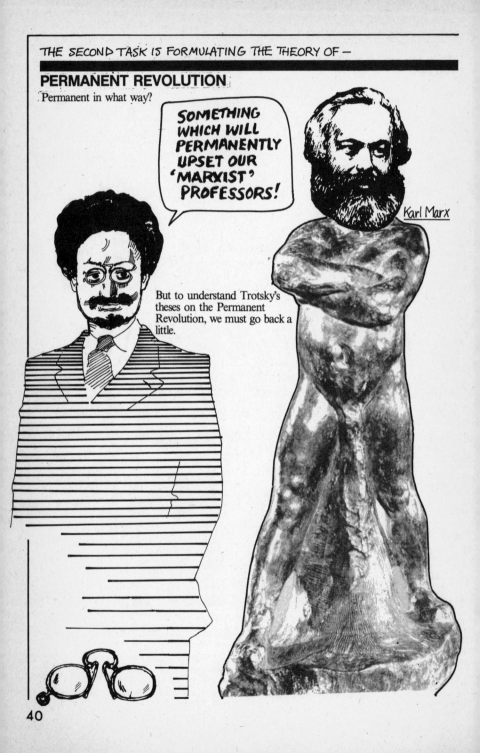

SOMETHING WHICH WILL PERMANENTLY UPSET OUR 'MARXIST' PROFESSORS!

Karl Marx

But to understand Trotsky's theses on the Permanent Revolution, we must go back a little.

In his preface to the *Critique of Political Economy* (1859) Marx had written . . .

No social order ever disappears until new material conditions—new forces of production—develop sufficiently to replace the old ones.

???

An industrially developed country shows a less developed one the image of its own future.

WHAT DOES THIS MEAN?

1. That all backward societies must, of necessity, go through the same stages of development as the advanced Western countries.

2. That for societies with a peasant majority, without democracy or political rights, the next stage of development must be capitalism and a *bourgeois* revolution.

41

G.V. Plekhanov.

This idea dominated Russian Marxism. Marxists believed that a Russian Revolution would bring the *bourgeoisie* to power. This was expressed in its clearest and most unequivocal form by the "father of Russian Marxism", G. V. Plekhanov. ❛ Russia stands at a crossroad on the way to capitalism, and all other issues are closed to her. In order to fight capitalism, only one way is left . . . to help it to grow as fast as possible. ❜

WHAT ABOUT THE WORKERS? WHERE DO WE FIT IN?

YOU DON'T!

And this was to remain the viewpoint of Menshevism.

Now Trotsky played a new card . . . Why do backward societies have to follow the same path as advanced ones? Trotsky's ideas marked a radical break with the views of Western European socialists. He stood the accepted Marxist dogma on its head.

Of course, Trotsky wasn't the first to use the words *permanent revolution*. Both Marx and Karl Kautsky had discussed the "permanence of the revolution". Nor was he the first to understand the non-bourgeois shape of the coming revolution. Parvus had interested him in the idea.

Here you may see what's very rare,
The world turn'd upside down
A tree and castle in the air ;
A man walk on his crown.

Poem from the English Revolution of 1642

But he was the first Marxist to develop a coherent theory of the Russian Revolution which stressed the leading role of the urban proletariat.

In *Results and Prospects* (1906) he expressed the ideas which he defended for the rest of his life.

BASIC POINTS OF PERMANENT REVOLUTION

Imperialism has established a world economy. Russian society was part of this world reality. This fact compelled it to develop a powerful and centralised State to defend itself from invaders. *"Even capitalism appeared as a child of the State."*

MY BABY!

1.

The immediate tasks confronting Russia are bourgeois-democratic:

1. to abolish semi-feudal relations in the countryside and emancipate the peasants

2. to elect a constituent assembly and proclaim a republic with the freedoms of voting, press, political parties, trade unions, etc.

3. self-determination for national minorities.

All this means destroying the Tsarist State.

2. Who's going to do it? The bourgeoisie?

No. The Russian bourgeoisie is timid, vacillating and weak, more frightened of workers and peasants than of the Tsar! And the bourgeoisie in Europe will support the Tsar because it wants to protect its enormous investments in Russia.

It is incapable of making a revolution even to further its own interests.

Who then will make the revolution? Workers and peasants—and it it will be despite and even against the bourgeoisie.

3 THE PEASANT?

Workers and peasants do not have the same social or historical weight. Numerically the peasants are the overwhelming majority. But they are dispersed, have no common outlook and have accepted subordination to an urban class.

The choice which will confront them: to stay under the Tsar or fight alongside the workers.

A DAY IN THE LIFE-OF A PEASANT

MY GOD — HENS ARE STUPID!

6AM. FEED THE HENS

7 TO 12. WORK IN THE FIELD

VODKA

12.15. LUNCH

12.30 – 7.0. WORK IN THE FIELD

8.0 – 11.0 BACK TO THE SHACK

PRAY THAT THE GOAT DOESN'T GET ILL, GO TO BED

4 THE WORKING CLASS?

It is the only social class capable of liberating Russia, of organising into revolutionary parties. But why should the workers fight if they are only going to hand over power to their enemy? They won't! Workers are not going to be satisfied just to put the bourgeoisie into power!

The democratic revolution will spill over immediately into a socialist one—and thereby become a permanent revolution.

A DAY IN THE LIFE - OF A WORKER

← WORKS

7.30. GO TO WORK, WITH ALL THE OTHERS.

WE ALL WORK UNTIL 12.30.

THEN WE ALL HAVE DINNER AND READ THE PAPERS AND HAVE A CHAT.

WAR IN THE BALKANS

5PM. WE ALL GO HOME.

THERE'LL BE A WAR!
AND I READ THAT —
NO-YOU'RE WRONG!

8PM. PERHAPS GO TO THE CLUB.

BED AT 11.0

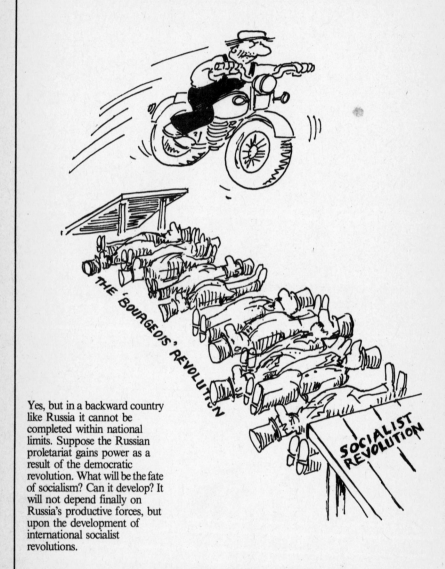

THE 'BOURGEOIS' REVOLUTION

SOCIALIST REVOLUTION

Yes, but in a backward country like Russia it cannot be completed within national limits. Suppose the Russian proletariat gains power as a result of the democratic revolution. What will be the fate of socialism? Can it develop? It will not depend finally on Russia's productive forces, but upon the development of international socialist revolutions.

THIS IS THE CRUCIAL DIFFERENCE BETWEEN TROTSKY AND STALIN!

Trotsky escapes from Siberia, once again, in February 1907. In Vienna, 1908, he starts his own newspaper, *Pravda*, struggles for the unity of the party and . . . plays chess with Alfred Adler, Freud's renegade disciple.

But his distance from both Mensheviks and Bolsheviks leaves him without any organisational anchor.

In his preface to the re-issue of *Results and Prospects* in post-revolutionary Russia in 1919, Trotsky summed up this period:

In maintaining the standpoint of the permanent revolution during a period of fifteen years, the author nevertheless fell into error in his estimation of the contending factions of the social-democratic movement. As both of them started out from the standpoint of bourgeois revolution, the author was of the opinion that the divergences existing between them would not be so deep as to justify a split. At the same time, he hoped that the further course of events would clearly prove the weakness and insignificance of Russian bourgeois democracy, on the one hand, and on the other, the objective impossibility of the proletariat limiting itself to a democratic programme. This he thought would remove the ground from under factional differences.

Having stood outside both of the factions in the period of emigration, the author did not fully appreciate the very important circumstance that in reality, along the line of disagreement between Bolsheviks and Mensheviks, there were being grouped inflexible revolutionaries on the one side and, on the other, elements which were becoming more and more opportunist and accommodating . . .'

1914-1917: WAR AND REVOLUTION

The First World War erupted in August 1914. It was a straightforward conflict between the major capitalist powers in Europe to determine which one would make more money on a global scale.

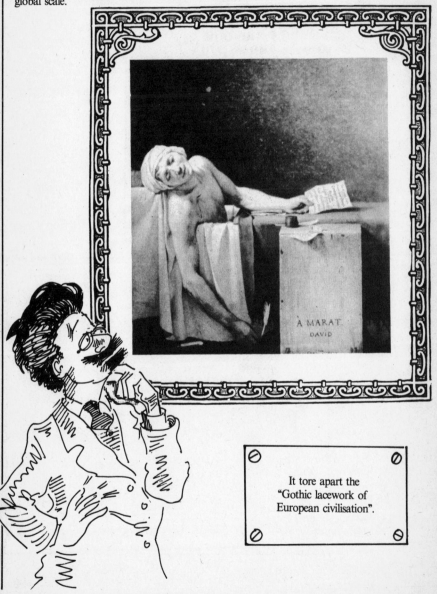

À MARAT
DAVID

It tore apart the "Gothic lacework of European civilisation".

Something else tore apart. The Second International, formed in 1889 by Europe's major socialist parties. Till 1914 (with the exception of the British Labour Party) it had pledged to resist militarism and war.

But on the first day of the war the International crumbled. Many of the Social-Democratic parties lined up with their own national ruling classes.

The revolutionary exiles from Tsarist Russia were thunderstruck. Most of them regarded what happened as a betrayal. And many of them now lost faith in bourgeois parliaments and parliamentary parties. A year after the outbreak of war Lenin proclaimed . . .

What Third International? Has he gone mad?

On 5 September 1915 in Zimmerwald, a little village in Switzerland, a conference of European socialists took place with 38 delegates from 11 countries. Most were pacifists. Only a few, led by Lenin, wanted to "turn the imperialist war into a civil war", a policy known as "revolutionary defeatism".

Lenin - on his way to the Zimmerwald conference

What's Lenin talking about? Simple! Let's use the disarray of international capitalism to open up a *second front* at home! Our enemy is at home! German revolutionaries had already been imprisoned for expressing similar views.

Trotsky disagrees with Lenin's call for civil war back home. Trotsky is asked to draw up the Zimmerwald Manifesto denouncing war. Lenin isn't satisfied, but votes for it. A committee is elected. This is the nucleus of the Third International.

HMMPH!

NASHIE SLOVO

THE PAPER FOR RED RUSSIAN EMIGRES   10 KOPEKS   1913

TROTSKY BECOMES EDITOR

I'm stunned, says Mum

Trotsky edits a ferocious anti-war newspaper from Paris called *Nashe Slovo* (Our Word). Its contributors will become famous over the next decade.

Alexandra Kollontai, writing from Scandinavia, will become Commissar for Public Welfare in 1917.

Alexandra Kollontai

G. Chicherin, London correspondent, will be Foreign Secretary of the Soviet Republic.

D. Ryazanov, Marxist scholar, will head the Marx-Engels Institue in Moscow. **A. Lozovsky** will head the Red Trade Union International.

D. Z. Manuilsky, **G. Y. Sokolnikov**, **N. N. Pokrovsky** and **Ivan Maisky** will all play important roles during and after the revolution. But some of these will not survive the infamous Stalinist purges.

Likeable

V. A. Antonov-Ovseenko, former Tsarist officer who led his detachment to side with the 1905 revolution, will command the Red Guards' famous assault on the Winter Palace in October 1917. Later joins Trotsky's Left Opposition, but capitulates to Stalin and serves as Consul in Spain. Recalled and executed 1938.

Karl Radek, member of the Polish, German and

| *by THE PEN* |

and Paris. Joins the Opposition to Stalin, deported to Siberia in 1928. Died or executed during imprisonment.

Swiss sections of the Second International before 1914, then a leading propagandist of the Comintern during Lenin's lifetime. Left Oppositionist to Stalin till Trotsky's deportation in 1929. Capitulates to

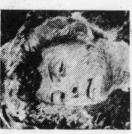

Karl Radek

Stalin and serves as Kremlin apologist. Convicted in the purge trial of 1937 and died during imprisonment.

Christian Rakovsky, a leader of the Balkan revolutionary movement before the Russian Revolution. Chairman of the Ukrainian Soviet in 1918 and then Soviet Ambassador to London

Woman attacked by rats in financial district

By GEORGE ARZT and CHRIS OLIVER

City exterminators today poison-spilled scattered food over a vacant lot in the financial district near City Hall where a woman reportedly fled in hysterics after being attacked and bitten by a pack of rats last night.

Rats poked their heads up through holes in the garbage-strewn lot on Ann Street between Broadway and Nassau Street as the Health Dept.'s Bureau of Pest Control crews scattered the bait. Police barred traffic in the immediate area.

● Full story
— See Page 5

The war drove many of these Russian intellectuals towards Bolshevism. Even Trotsky, self-confident, aware of his own talents, is forced to acknowledge that things are moving Lenin's way in Russia. Strikes, mutiny and defeatism at the front, food shortages, peasant unrest. In March 1916 Trotsky publishes a pro-Bolshevik text.

One ought not to and one need not share the sectarian narrow-mindedness of (the Bolsheviks) . . . but it cannot be denied that . . . in Russia, in the thick of political action, so-called Leninism is freeing itself from its sectarian features . . . and that the workers groups connected with Lenin's paper *Social Democrat* are now in Russia the only active and consistent internationalist force . . . For those internationalists that belong to no faction there is no way out but to merge with the Leninists, which in most cases means joining the Leninist organisation . . .

Russian revolutionaries had been hounded out of all countries because of their opposition to the war. Many, like Lenin, utilised Swiss neutrality and took refuge in Zurich.

Trotsky was expelled from France as a "suspect alien" and eventually came to the United States. He was in New York 10 weeks when the Russian Revolution broke out. Lenin, Trotsky and other exiles rush back as best they can!

16 April 1917: Lenin arrives at the Finland Station,
St. Petersburg (now renamed Petrograd). His
speech astounds his audience and the Bolsheviks.

N. N. Sukhanov, the eminent Menshevik historian, records that, "Lenin's
remarks resounded like a thunderbolt from a clear blue sky . . . it stunned
and confused even the most faithful of his disciples." But why?

Some days later, L. B. Kamenev, one of the staunchest Bolsheviks, wrote in the official Bolshevik paper, *Pravda:*

L. Kamenev

As for the general schema of comrade Lenin, it seems to us unacceptable, in that it starts from the assumption that the bourgeois democratic revolution is ended and counts upon an immediate transformation of this revolution into a socialist revolution.

I AGREE WITH KAMENEV!

Well, well! Has Lenin finally become a Trotskyist? Let's see.

DUAL POWER

Lenin, in April, called for the seizure of power by the working class. That's why so many loyal Bolsheviks were shocked. Lenin had abandoned the orthodox dogma. Lenin was now faced with the task of bringing the Bolsheviks into line with his new position— one which was virtually identical with Trotsky's idea of Permanent Revolution.

As in 1905, the February Revolution immediately elected a Soviet of Workers' and Soldiers' Deputies. Almost overnight it was the *only* organisation with effective power. Everyone knew it.

Tsereteli

But the Soviet leadership—Mensheviks, Social-Revolutionaries and others, including some Bolsheviks—believed it was a "law of Marxism" that this power should be transferred to the liberal bourgeoisie. I. G. Tsereteli, a Menshevik leader in the Soviet, explained the necessity of compromise with the bourgeoisie:

"It's true that we have all the power, and the government would go if we lifted a finger, but that would mean disaster for the revolution."

And so, blinded by the orthodox Marxist dogma of "bourgeois revolution", the Soviet leaders actually begged the liberal leaders of the Provisional Government—a 'government' in name only—to take power! This is how Dual Power emerged.

Trotsky's predictions had come true! Here was the absurd contradiction of victorious workers handing over power to a "weak, vacillating bourgeoisie".

63

Trotsky arrives in Petrograd in early May—and goes straight to the Tauride Palace where the Soviet is in session.

Remember three commands: distrust the bourgeoisie; control your own leaders; and rely on your revolutionary strength!

Mensheviks and other socialist leaders of the Soviet dissociate themselves sharply from Trotsky. They would continue to support a bourgeois coalition government. Within a few weeks Trotsky and his Mezhraiontsy group had joined with the Bolsheviks.

From May to October 1917 an intense struggle goes on inside the Soviet between moderate socialists and Bolsheviks. Lenin calls for an end to the war waged by capitalists for capitalist interests.

July 1917 sees a mass uprising in Petrograd. Lenin and the Bolshevik leadership regard it as premature, but refuse to stand aside as neutrals.

VOLTAIRE

The uprising is defeated. The socialist executive of the Soviet disarms the workers with the help of the hated Cossacks. Bolsheviks are attacked.

Trotsky is arrested. Lenin is accused of being a "German spy" and goes into hiding.

A. F. Kerensky, the socialist Prime Minister of the Provisional Government, conspires with his Commander-in-Chief, General Kornilov, to overthrow the Soviets.
Kerensky backs down at the last minute, 9 September 1917, but not Kornilov.

BULLSHIT!

I, General Kornilov, son of a Cossack peasant, cannot betray Russia into the hands of the ancestral enemy, the German . . . It's time to hang German supporters and spies with Lenin at their head, and to disperse the Soviet of Workers' and Soldiers' Deputies so that it shall never re-assemble. I am shifting the cavalry corps so as to bring it up to Petrograd.
Kornilov

Sailors from the Kronstadt Soviet visit Trotsky in prison.

Kerensky re-arms the Red Guards and begs Bolshevik agitators to get Kornilov's soldiers to mutiny. Bolshevik propaganda and agitation defeats Kornilov: the would-be dictator finds he is a general without an army! His soldiers desert without a shot being fired.

COOOMME BAAACKK!!

I COULD HAVE TOLD HIM THAT!

BOLSHEVISM IS VINDICATED

Bolsheviks obtain a majority of votes in the Petrograd Soviet, October 1917, and Trotsky is elected President. In Moscow, and elsewhere throughout Russia, Bolsheviks gain majorities in the Soviets. This build-up of popular democratic support was, for Lenin and Trotsky, the green light for a workers' insurrection.

Land, bread and peace, the slogan of Bolshevik agitation, found a ready response. Conditions had become grim, as John Reed the American journalist vividly described.

It was dark from three o'clock in the afternoon to ten in the morning. Robberies and house-breaking increased. In apartment houses men took turns at all-night duty, armed with loaded rifles. This was under the provisional government. Week by week food became scarcer. The daily allowance of bread fell from a pound-and-a-half to a pound, then three-quarters, half and a quarter-pound. Towards the end there was a week without any bread at all.

23 October 1917: Lenin, in disguise, returns from Finland to Petrograd, and appears before a secret session of the Bolshevik Central Committee, which includes Trotsky. The decision is taken for an immediate revolutionary seizure of power. Only two vote against—Zinoviev and Kamenev.

Much time has been lost . . . the question is very urgent and the decisive moment is near. *The majority is now with us. The situation has become entirely ripe for the transfer of power . . . Insurrection: we cannot wait any longer.*
Lenin

Before history, before the international proletariat, before the Russian revolution and the Russian working class, we have no right to stake the whole future on the card of an armed uprising.
Kamenev

Zinoviev and Kamenev oppose the insurrection in a published article—and even reveal the date! Lenin wants to expel them as "strikebreakers" for this. But the Central Committee refuses.

THE OCTOBER REVOLUTION

On 25 October (or 7 November, New Style calendar) 1917 the Military Revolutionary Committee of the Petrograd Soviet launched a successful insurrection. Lenin's influence was decisive. But who organised the insurrection? Let Stalin tell us . . .

The entire labour of practical organisation of the insurrection was placed under the immediate direction of the president of the Petrograd Soviet, comrade Trotsky. It can be stated with certainty, that the party owes the rapid coming over of the garrison into the camp of the soviets and the skilful work of the Revolutionary Military Committee above all and essentially to Comrade Trotsky (Pravda, 6 November 1917).
Joseph Stalin

Lenin and Trotsky are trying to get to sleep on the floor of the Bolshevik Headquarters in the Smolny Institute. Trotsky suggests that the new government should be named a Council of People's Commisars. Lenin agrees, but wonders . . .

Subsequent elections, during the All-Russia Congress of Soviets show a clear Bolshevik majority. 14 Bolsheviks, 7 Socialist-Revolutionaries and 3 Mensheviks on the Praesidium of the Soviets. The defeated parties begin to walk out. The Left and Centre Mensheviks demand a coalition government. When the Bolsheviks refuse, Martov and others lead a walkout.

Martov

6 *Our rising has been victorious. Now they tell us: Renounce your victory, yield, make a compromise. With whom? With those miserable little groups that have left or with those that make these proposals? . . . Nobody in the whole of Russia follows them any more. You are miserable, isolated individuals. You are bankrupt. You have played out your role. Go where you belong: to the dustheap of history.* 9

TROTSKY from the 'History of the Russian Revolution'

78

After the October Revolution, the Bolsheviks treated the Tsarist generals with generosity. Something rarely acknowledged by bourgeois historians.

The revolution made the mistake of showing magnanimity to the leader of the Cossack attack (General Krasnov). He should have been shot on the spot. At the end of a few days he recovered his liberty, after giving his word of honour never to take arms against the revolution. But what value can promises of honour have towards enemies of fatherland and property? He was to go off to put the Don region to fire and sword.

from 'YEAR ONE OF THE RUSSIAN REVOLUTION' by Victor Serge

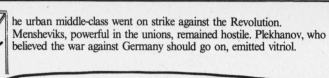

The urban middle-class went on strike against the Revolution. Mensheviks, powerful in the unions, remained hostile. Plekhanov, who believed the war against Germany should go on, emitted vitriol.

The Bolshevik bandits are a revolting mixture of Utopian idealists, imbeciles, traitors and anarchist provocateurs . . . We must not only master but crush this vermin, drown it in blood. That is the price of Russia's safety.
Plekhanov

The "Father of Russian Marxism" has become the custodian of the Russian bourgeoisie!

Sabotage and counter-revolution are not the only problems. The Bolshevik military leader Antonov-Oveenko describes the influence of alcohol on the Petrograd regiments.

'*A wild and unexampled orgy spread over Petrograd . . . We tried to stop them by walling up the entrances. The crowd penetrated through the windows, forced out the bars and grabbed the stocks.*
An attempt was made to flood the cellars with water. The fire brigades sent to do this themselves got drunk . . . The whole city was infected by the drinking madness. At last the Council of People's Commisars appointed a special commisar, endowed him with emergency powers, and gave him a strong escort. But the commissar, too, proved unreliable . . . Only after an intense effort was this alcoholic lunacy overcome.'

81

Bigger problems confront the Revolution than alcohol. The Allied Powers are desperately against Russia signing a separate peace with Germany. But Bolshevik foreign policy is clear—an immediate armistice with Germany is the aim.

Trotsky, named as Commissar of Foreign Affairs, and emissaries of Soviet Russia arrive at Brest-Litovsk to negotiate peace at the end of November 1917. They confront the Generals, Princes and politicans of the German and Austro-Hungarian Empires.

The peace delegation at Brest-Litovsk distributed revolutionary pamphlets to the German soldiers.

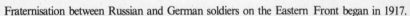

Fraternisation between Russian and German soldiers on the Eastern Front began in 1917.

Deutsche und russische Soldaten verbrüdern sich 1917

That was only a foretaste of the propaganda to follow. Bolshevik leaders were all agreed to use every means of agitation and propaganda to encourage the rising tide of socialist revolution in Germany.

But the Bolshevik Central Committee were divided over the crucial question, whether or not to make concessions to the German armies occupying areas of Russia. There are three positions.

Lenin sees Trotsky's position as attractive but too risky. Trotsky's resolution is passed by the Central Committee. Lenin is in the minority.

Trotsky returns to Brest-Litovsk and uses it to address the oppressed of the world. But the Germans launch a new offensive in February 1918. The Bolshevik Central Committee meets. Trotsky goes over to Lenin, and with this majority, acceptance of peace goes ahead, 3 March 1918.

Was Lenin crazy? Think of Mao Tsetung. His Long March in 1934 was a comparable strategy.

Brest-Litovsk showed that the Bolshevik Party was extremely healthy. The three sides of the peace question were publicly debated in the pages of *Pravda*. This is what is meant by "politics in command".

THE REVOLUTION'S FINEST HOUR

This party, so disciplined and so little encumbered by an abstract fetishism for democracy, still in these grave hours respects its norms of internal democracy. It puts its recognised leader in a minority; Lenin's tremendous personal authority does not hinder the militants in the Central Committee from standing up to him and energetically maintaining their point of view; the most important questions are settled by vote, often by small majorities, to which the minorities are willing to defer without abandoning their ideas.

Lenin, when in the minority, submits while waiting for events to prove him right, and continues his propaganda without breaking discipline ... Neither gossip nor intrigue nor personalities play any important part in what is said. The militants talk politics, without trying to wound or to discredit comrades on the opposing side ...

Victor Serge

THE INCREDIBLE BECOMES REAL THE IMPOSSIBLE BECOMES PROBABLE

HE CIVIL WAR BEGINS

The infant Soviet Republic, threatened by German armies in the Ukraine, faces another big problem. Civil war. The Tsarist White generals prepare a counter-revolution. The Allied Powers, angered by the Bolshevik peace negotiations, are ready to support the Whites.

The so-called Civil War in Russia saw the Bolsheviks fighting not only against the forces led by White generals: Denikin, Wrangel, Yudenich, Kolchak. But the Whites were aided by 50 thousand Allied soldiers. British, American, Italian, Serb, French, Czech, Poles and Japanese troops joined the holy crusade against the Red Republic. Their aim is to crush the world's first workers' state.

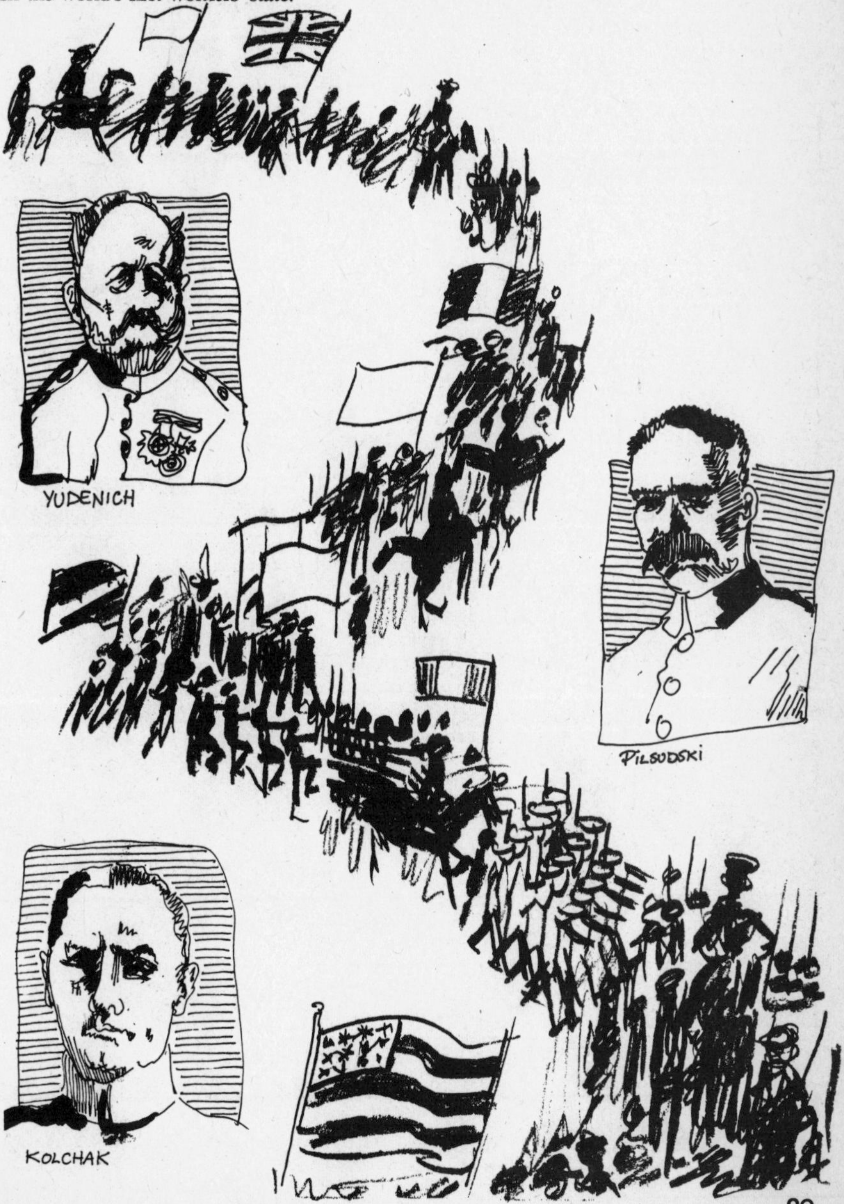

YUDENICH

PILSUDSKI

KOLCHAK

Trotsky was given the responsibility of organising the Red Army. Why Trotsky? Because his ability had already been proven by the military success of the October uprising.

▬▬▬▬▬▬▬▬▬▬▬▬▬▬

Trotsky proposes that some Tsarist officers should be used by the Red Army which urgently needs experienced military men.

Many ex-Tsarist officers desert the Red Army to join the Whites. But a greater number are won over to the Revolution.

The Whites commit many atrocities. When they massacre the workers of Kazan, the Bolsheviks reply in kind. Of course, there is an outcry against Bolshevik 'cruelty'.

' The only unpardonable sin which the Russian working class can commit at this moment is that of indulgence towards its class enemies. '

TROTSKY — from 'MY LIFE'

Trotsky moulds the Red Army into a fighting force without equal. In the years of Civil War and foreign intervention (1918-21) he is the supreme strategist of the Revolution.

Right: Trotsky with his armoured train

THESE ARE MY ORDERS, MEN. I WILL ATTACK FIRST — BUT I WANT THE RED ARMY TO COVER ME!

His special armoured train takes him to the front and he participates in the battles. Irresponsible? No. Leaders should be seen as capable of defending the Revolution when the occasion demands it.

In 1919, at the height of the Civil War, the Communist International—Lenin's self-proclaimed Third International—is founded. In his war train Trotsky drafts a manifesto which is unanimously adopted.

IF HE DOESN'T HURRY UP IT'LL BE THE **FOURTH** INTERNATIONAL!

LONG LIVE THE THIRD INTERNATIONAL

Hastily thrown together, the First Congress represented some thirty-odd small groups sympathetic to Bolshevism.

MEANWHILE IN GERMANY . . .

The outbreak of war had deeply divided the German socialist movement, and particularly the big, influential Social-Democratic Party (SDP). On the brink of defeat—and following the abdication of Kaiser Wilhelm II, 9 November 1918—the German General Staff called on the SDP to form a republican government. The most nationalist elements in the SDP, the most respectful of state authority, such as Friedrich Ebert and Gustav Noske, responded willingly.

Friedrich Ebert

Gustav Noske

HELP!

But German workers, soldiers and sailors were as restless as the Russians had been in February 1917. Soviets—Workers' Councils—had sprung up independently in the major urban areas of Germany. Large numbers of workers were ready for battle. But where was the leadership? Might it come from the German Communist Party which was itself uncertain of whole-hearted popular support? Only one thing was sure. Ebert, Noske and the German Generals were not going to allow a 'Bolshevik' revolution in Germany. The scene was set for betrayal and a blood bath.

In street battles, December 1918 to January 1919, Noske's troops savagely stamped down the workers and effectively ended the possibility of revolution.

Gustav Noske says:

If these crowds instead of being led by prattlers, had possessed resolute leaders, conscious of where they were going, they would have been masters of Berlin . . .

AR COMMUNISM

The Civil War proved very costly. It killed off a generation of the most politically conscious workers. It ruined Russia's economy. Apart from war deaths, some 9 million perished in 1919-20 of cold, famine and disease.

CONDITIONS DURING THE CIVIL WAR

"War Communism" met the economic emergency by imposing tighter state control, more expropriations and confiscation of grain from the hard-pressed peasantry. This policy meant a virtual militarisation of the Soviet Republic with the Bolshevik party as the "General Staff". It was supposed to be a temporary measure.

In 1920 Trotsky submitted a list of proposals to the Central Committee to change gear and restore an element of the free market.

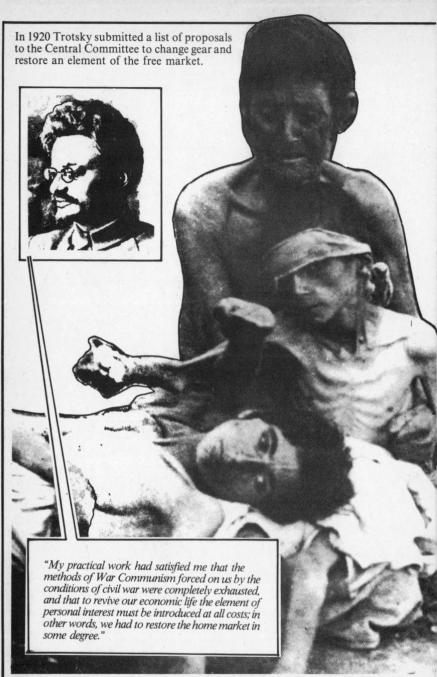

"*My practical work had satisfied me that the methods of War Communism forced on us by the conditions of civil war were completely exhausted, and that to revive our economic life the element of personal interest must be introduced at all costs; in other words, we had to restore the home market in some degree.*"

This position is rejected by Lenin and the Central Committee.

THE KRONSTADT UPRISING: 1921

The Kronstadt Soviet was a strong naval fortress on an island off Petrograd. Its sailors were famous as the vanguard of the Revolution and loyal Bolshevik supporters.

Why did they revolt in March, 1921?

Many of the sailors, as "sons of peasants" wanted an end to grain confiscations. They demanded a free market and democratic freedoms which the emergency laws of War Communism had abolished.

A letter from home

THEY TOOK MY GRAIN SON – WHAT ARE YOU GOING TO DO?

But Trotsky, Lenin and the Bolshevik Central Committee do not listen. Before the ice can melt, they send the Red Army commanded by Tukhachevsky to crush the sailors' mutiny. The Kronstadt tragedy will haunt Trotsky for the rest of his life.

Tukhachevsky

Many Communists, like Victor Serge, were sympathetic to the Kronstadt demands, But Serge explains why he and many others decided to back the Party against the sailors.

"If the Bolshevik dictatorship fell, it was only a short step to chaos, and through chaos to a peasant rising, the massacre of the Communists, the return of the emigres, and in the end, through sheer force of events, another dictatorship, this time anti-proletarian."
Victor Serge, *Memoirs of a Revolutionary.*

THE 10TH CONGRESS OF THE COMMUNIST PARTY

The 10th Congress opens in Moscow while Kronstadt fights to the last man. Lenin proposes a *New Economic Policy* (NEP). He wants to abolish War Communism, to end grain requisitions and permit a limited free market.

Lenin defined the *New Economic Policy* as "State Capitalism". Private entrepreneurs (Nepmen) made profits in the towns. In the countryside, rich peasants (kulaks) prospered. NEP was tough on workers and poor peasants.

NEP was opposed inside the Bolshevik party by the leaders of the Workers Opposition. This faction, led by the Commissar of Labour, A. G. Shliapnikov, Alexandra Kollontai and others, demanded the management of production by the unions.

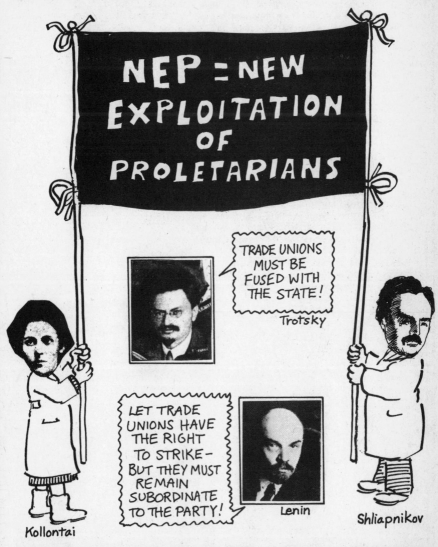

NEP = NEW EXPLOITATION OF PROLETARIANS

TRADE UNIONS MUST BE FUSED WITH THE STATE!
Trotsky

LET TRADE UNIONS HAVE THE RIGHT TO STRIKE — BUT THEY MUST REMAIN SUBORDINATE TO THE PARTY!
Lenin

Kollontai

Shliapnikov

The 10th Congress gave a rough time to oppositionists within the Bolshevik party.

LOOKING BACK — AND AHEAD

By 1921 the Bolsheviks had banned all opposition parties. This happened, understandably enough, during the Civil War. The main opposition parties, including left ones, had either collaborated with the Whites—or threatened to do so.

But the 10th Congress went further and banned factions. If you ban other parties, it seems inevitable to curtail dissent in your own. Both Lenin and Trotsky defended this measure, insisting it was temporary.

The Civil War had been won by 1921. There was no real threat to the Soviet state. Why ban factions? Because it seemed necessary to Lenin and Trotsky that the 'liberal' measures of NEP must be imposed even at the cost of silencing dissent within the Bolshevik ranks.

In reality, the emergency measures of War Communism, and then NEP, had actually strengthened the apparatus of the state, the party and the bureaucracy, at the "temporary" cost of democracy. If this apparatus fell into the wrong hands, Soviet democracy would be in real danger!

Lenin understood this. And so did Trotsky. In 1923 and later Trotsky warned: "We must not build socialism by the bureaucratic road, we must not create a socialist society by administrative orders . . . bureaucratisation is a deadly enemy of socialism . . ." (*Izvestia,* 2 June 1925)

The revolutionary tide had ebbed in Europe. But the European Communist parties, though often weak, refused to recognise this fact. At the Third Congress of the Communist International, in the summer of 1921, Lenin and Trotsky developed their concept of the United Front. They were resisted by the ultra-radicals, like Zinoviev, Bukharin and the Hungarian Bela Kun.

Bukharin

Bela Kun

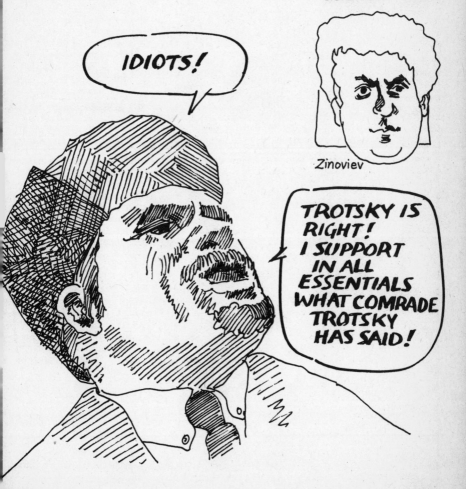

IDIOTS!

Zinoviev

TROTSKY IS RIGHT! I SUPPORT IN ALL ESSENTIALS WHAT COMRADE TROTSKY HAS SAID!

But what had Comrade Trotsky said?

1. The Communist parties in Europe are not immediately presented with revolutionary opportunities.

2. They have still to win over a majority of the workers, without whom there can be no revolution in Western countries.

3. Lenin said, and Trotsky agreed, that " . . . to assure the victory of Socialism it is necessary to have the united forces of the workers of several highly developed countries." This must be accomplished through the *United Front.*

What is the United Front?

Unity for common objectives between Communists and trade unions, socialist and Social-Democratic workers' organisations. Only by working together with such organisations would the Communist parties be able to convince workers of the correctness of communist ideas.

In essence, the United Front is the continuation of Trotsky's belief in Permanent Revolution. It also reveals, once again, the typical feature of Trotsky's non-factionalism. To put it simply, "March separately, but strike together!"

The Comintern voted for the United Front policy in 1921, and it was re-affirmed at its 4th Congress in 1922.

We shall see later what happened to the United Front strategy.

THE RISE OF STALIN

The 11th Party Congress in March 1922 was the last Lenin attended. After this Congress, the Central Committee elected Stalin as General Secretary of the Communist Party.

This cook will only cook peppery dishes!
Lenin

Lenin might have been uneasy. But no one dreamed that Stalin might one day take over.

In May 1922 Lenin falls seriously ill, paralysed by a stroke.

107

During Lenin's illness, the Party leadership passes to Zinoviev, Kamenev and Stalin. This 'triumvirate' holds the key positions. Kamenev was married to Trotsky's sister. This didn't prevent him from siding with Zinoviev and Stalin against Trotsky!

Trotsky's position as Chairman of the Military Revolutionary Council is an honorary one. His abilities are not sufficiently used; he is being side-tracked and not given any key work in the Party apparatus.

Slowly but surely Stalin plants his men as secretaries throughout the Party organisation to gain control over it. He works out changes in the governmental structure.

Lenin, during his illness, has time to think.

OUR WORKERS STATE
IS DEFORMED — THE
WEIGHT OF BUREAUCRACY
IS TOO GREAT — THE
DIVISION BETWEEN
TROTSKY AND STALIN
SPELLS DISASTER...

Lenin's last battle was to be against Stalin. While the Party prepares for its
March 1923 12th Congress, Lenin plans:
   1. to censure Stalin for ordering a Red Army invasion of Georgia above
the heads of the Politburo
  2. to remove Stalin as General Secretary.

Illness again prevents Lenin from going into action. On 21 January 1924 Lenin dies.

Trotsky, on his way to Sukhum in the Caucasus to recover from an infection, receives a telegram from Stalin. "The Politburo thinks that because of the state of your health you must proceed to Sukhum." Trotsky does not attend Lenin's funeral.

Lenin had written a "Last Testament" which made one important demand: *Stalin should be removed as General Secretary.* The Politburo decided to keep quiet about the Testament. Despite bitter protests from Lenin's widow, Krupskaya, the Party Congress was not told.

' TROTSKY IS THE MOST ABLE MAN ON THE CENTRAL COMMITTEE BUT HAS TOO FAR-REACHING SELF CONFIDENCE '

' STALIN IS TOO RUDE. REMOVE STALIN FROM THE POSITION OF GENERAL SECRETARY '

' BUKHARIN IS THE PARTY'S MOST VALUABLE THEORETICIAN BUT IS TOO SCHOLASTIC '

' THE OCTOBER EPISODE OF ZINOVIEV AND KAMENEV WAS NOT ACCIDENTAL... '

PUBLISH THE TESTAMENT!

Krupskaya

Trotsky accepted Party discipline once the decision was taken to suppress Lenin's instructions.

111

Trotsky did worse. He allowed himself to be talked into a compromise with the 'Triumvirate'. He did not speak up on the Georgian question. He did not attack Stalin. His silence would prove costly.

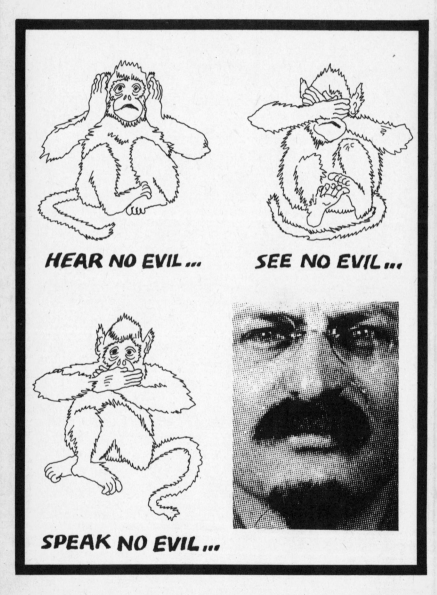

HEAR NO EVIL...   SEE NO EVIL...

SPEAK NO EVIL...

Stalin was re-elected General Secretary and became, in effect, the Party's master.

One day, sometime later, Trotsky meets a friend who has just lost his position at the War Ministry.

WHAT'S GOING ON?

Trotsky, like other clear-headed Bolsheviks, understood that a real decline in class-consciousness had taken place. Revolution was defeated in Europe. In Russia, it degenerated. A new social layer arose and strengthened its grip on society as a whole. Who are they?

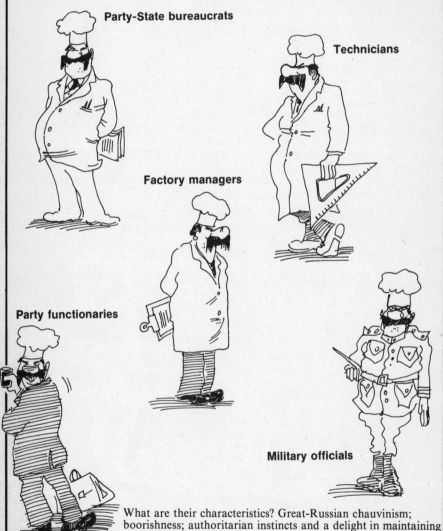

Party-State bureaucrats

Technicians

Factory managers

Party functionaries

Military officials

What are their characteristics? Great-Russian chauvinism; boorishness; authoritarian instincts and a delight in maintaining their material privileges.

THE LEFT OPPOSITION

Trotsky had not been idle. In October 1923 the struggle for Party democracy had begun. *The Letter of the Forty-Six* was a statement issued by 46 prominent Bolsheviks against the Party leadership. Their letter demanded better economic planning, freedom of criticism, debate, and a new emergency Party conference to review the situation.

Who were among the '46'—and what eventually happened to them?

E. A. Preobrazhensky: economist and Politburo member (liquidated 1937).

V. A. Antonov-Ovseenko: chief Political Commissar of the Red Army (liquidated 1938).

N. I. Muralov: Commander of the Moscow garrison (liquidated 1937).

T. V. Sapronov: a leader of the Workers' Opposition (liquidated 1938).

The Letter was suppressed by the Central Committee. Trotsky was censured and the 46 were warned that they were breaching the 1921 ban on factions.

THE SLANDER CAMPAIGN BEGINS

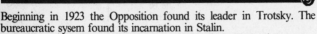

Beginning in 1923 the Opposition found its leader in Trotsky. The bureaucratic sysem found its incarnation in Stalin.

Beginning in 1923 an agitational campaign unlimited in its violence was launched against Trotsky. Old disagreements with Lenin, dating back from 1904 to 1915, were dug up under Stalin's orders and used to create the heretic myth of 'Trotskyism'. Trotsky was slandered as a criminal anti-Leninist.

HY DIDN'T TROTSKY "DO MORE"?

Trotsky, in 1923, was still popular as the organiser of the Red Army. Should he have attempted a military coup? It went against Trotsky's beliefs simply to replace bureaucratic rule by army rule.

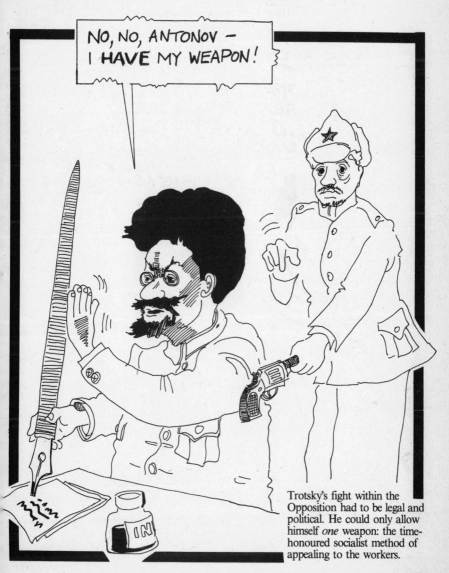

Trotsky's fight within the Opposition had to be legal and political. He could only allow himself *one* weapon: the time-honoured socialist method of appealing to the workers.

In May 1924 the 13th Party Congress condemns the pro-democracy faction and Trotsky in particular.

1924: Trotsky writes *The Lessons of October* in reply to his critics, who respond with more slander and by removing him from his position as Commissar of War.

1925: the Central Committee removes Trotsky from the Military Revolutionary Council and forbids him to engage in any new debates. But the Stalinists take the anti-Trotsky campaign to the country as a whole.

Thus, with the badges of infamy stuck over the badges of his fame, with cries of denunciation ringing in his ears, gagged and forbidden even to defend himself, he left the Commissariat and the army which he had led for seven long and fateful years
Isaac Deutscher: The Prophet Unarmed

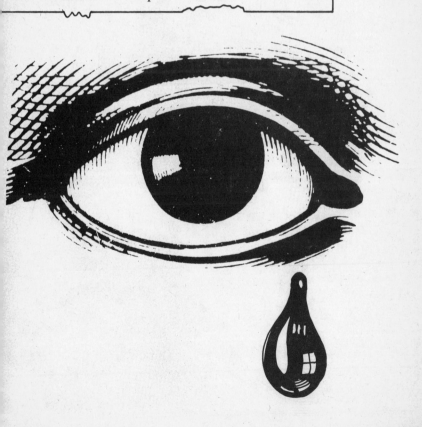

Adolph Abramovich Joffe, a veteran revolutionary and emissary of the Soviet republic to China, Japan, Europe, and an old friend of Trotsky's committed suicide in 1927. He was depressed by the growing degeneration he saw around him. He left behind a last letter addressed to Trotsky:

Joffe

I have always believed that you lacked Lenin's unbending will, his unwillingness to yield, his readiness even to remain alone on the path that he thought right in the anticipation of a future majority, of a future recognition by every one of the rightness of his path. Politically, you were always right, beginning with 1905, and I told you repeatedly that with my own ears I heard Lenin admit that even in 1905, you, and not he, were right. One does not lie before his death, and now I repeat this to you . . . But you have often abandoned your rightness for the sake of an overvalued agreement, or compromise. This is a mistake. I repeat: politically you have always been right, and now more right than ever. Some day the party will realise it, and history will not fail to accord recognition . . . You are right, but the guarantee of the victory of your rightness lies in nothing but the extreme unwillingness to yield, the strictest straightforwardness, the absolute rejection of all compromise; in this lay the very secret of Lenin's victories . . .

120

THE THEORY OF SOCIALISM IN ONE COUNTRY

At the 14th Party Congress in 1926 Trotsky remained silent as the senior Triumvirs, Zinoviev and Kamenev, split with Stalin who forms a new faction with Bukharin and the Right Wing.

The issues are important. Stalin proclaims his theory of "socialism in one country". This means putting the safety of Russia's own economic development first, above an international policy of revolution. Bukharin tells the wealthier peasants, the kulaks, "Enrich yourselves!"

ENRICH YOURSELVES!

Zinoviev and Kamenev, too late, realise that Stalin has cleverly let them take the blame for all internal and foreign failures. Outflanked, Zinoviev reminds the Congress delegates of Lenin's Testament, while Krupskaya and others demand a free debate.

Trotsky is wooed by both sides. He remains aloof. During the Central Committee and Politburo meetings he reads French novels. Disgusted by them all, he shows his contempt for their method of debate.

LOST ILLUSIONS

BY HONORÉ BALZAC

But he is tragically wrong. If he had thrown his weight behind Zinoviev and his supporters, the anti-Stalinist opposition would have been enormously strengthened.

The hand that wields the biggest whip is Stalin's. He now has total organisational control over the Party. But he needs political alliances to pursue his bureaucratic, agrarian policies. He needs a head that can think.

Bukharin offers his!

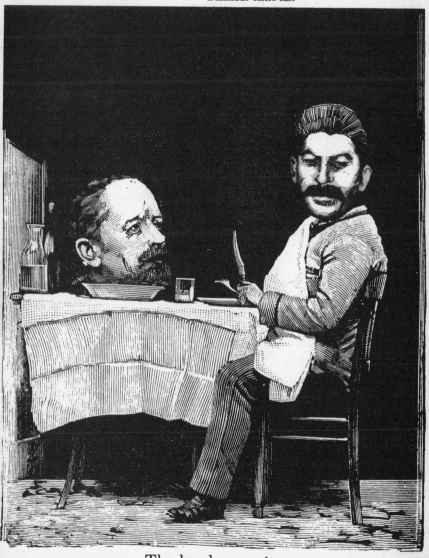

The head on a plate.

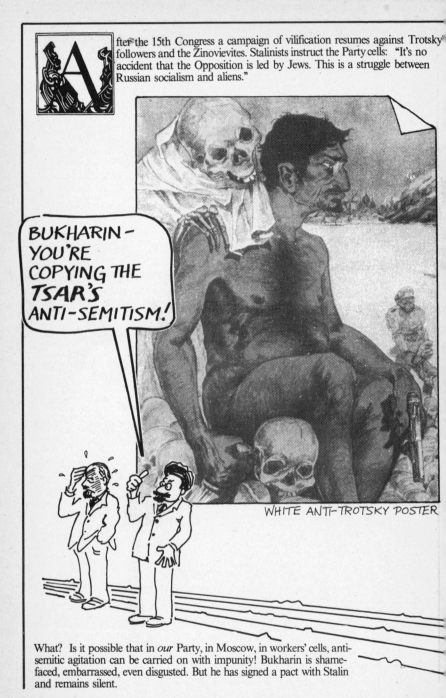

After the 15th Congress a campaign of vilification resumes against Trotsky's followers and the Zinovievites. Stalinists instruct the Party cells: "It's no accident that the Opposition is led by Jews. This is a struggle between Russian socialism and aliens."

BUKHARIN - YOU'RE COPYING THE TSAR'S ANTI-SEMITISM!

WHITE ANTI-TROTSKY POSTER

What? Is it possible that in *our* Party, in Moscow, in workers' cells, anti-semitic agitation can be carried on with impunity! Bukharin is shame-faced, embarrassed, even disgusted. But he has signed a pact with Stalin and remains silent.

124

In April 1926 Trotsky meets privately with Zinoviev and Kamenev who admit plotting with Stalin, fabricating charges and so on. *"We were blind. Stalin is sly, perverse, cruel."* Zinoviev and Kamenev go over to the Left Opposition, in an embarrassing about-face, when they are already isolated. Trotsky is not too optimistic.

YOU KNOW WHAT THOSE TWO ARE LIKE !

Meanwhile, Stalin's bureaucratic policies gain ground, and there are two more disasters on the international front.

THE 1926 BRITISH GENERAL STRIKE

British trade-union leaders, with whom Stalin has collaborated, capitulate and surrender the General Strike to Prime Minister Stanley Baldwin.

Stanley Baldwin.

Trotsky's book, *Where Is Britain Going?*, is widely distributed. It is a ferocious attack on Fabian socialism.

"British pigeon-fanciers, by means of artificial selection, achieve special varieties, with a continually shortening beak . . . One can say that the political art of the British bourgeois consists in shortening the revolutionary beak of the proletariat, and so not allowing him to pierce the shell of the capitalist state . . . If we look at Ramsay Macdonald, Thomas, Mr. and Mrs. Snowden, we have to confess that the work of the bourgeoisie in selecting short-billed and soft-billed has been crowned with astonishing success."

126

THE 1927 SHANGHAI MASSACRE

Stalin's guidance led to another debacle in China. Soviet and Comintern agents, on orders from Stalin, instructed the Chinese Communist Party to subordinate itself to Chiang Kaishek and the bourgeois Kuomintang Party. With some hesitation the Chinese Party accepted this. Chiang Kaishek used its passivity to carry out a massacre of Communist workers in Shanghai and Canton.

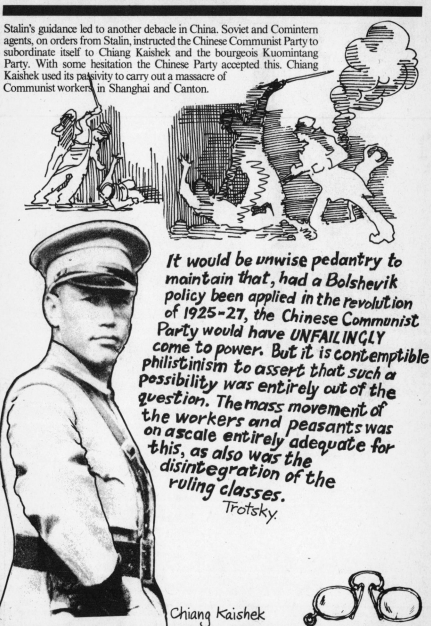

It would be unwise pedantry to maintain that, had a Bolshevik policy been applied in the revolution of 1925-27, the Chinese Communist Party would have UNFAILINGLY come to power. But it is contemptible philistinism to assert that such a possibility was entirely out of the question. The mass movement of the workers and peasants was on a scale entirely adequate for this, as also was the disintegration of the ruling classes.
Trotsky.

Chiang Kaishek

THE LAST FIGHT INSIDE THE PARTY: 1926-1927

For 18 months following July 1926 Trotsky threw himself into the struggle against Stalinism. At its height, the united Left Opposition had a membership of 8,000 Bolsheviks inside the Party. On the outcome of this fight depended the fate of the Revolution. Yet it was a struggle in which the masses were not directly involved.

Clandestine meetings of the Left Opposition took place in workers' homes, in the frost outside Moscow. Almost like old times.

Almost, but not quite!

SUMMARY OF THE LEFT OPPOSITION'S PLATFORM

On the Economic Front

Improve the conditions of urban workers; raise wages; phase out overtime work; improve housing; increase unemployment-benefits; equal pay for equal work in relation to women; election of trade-union officials; independence of factory-committees and trade unions from management at all levels.

On the Peasant Front

In the class struggle in the countryside, the Party must stand at the head of farm-labourers, poor and middle-peasants against exploitation by the kulaks.

On the Party Front

Officials outnumber workers within the Party. Figures in January 1927 show 462,000 officials and 445,000 workers. Degeneration of the Party regime is giving birth to a new caste of bureaucrats. Restore inner-Party democracy. End the situation of Party education being confined to democracy. End the situation of Party education being confined to Opposition-baiting. Stop repression and threats against dissidents.

On the International Front

Disasters in China and elsewhere are the results of a wrong political line being followed by the Comintern. Proper aid and advice must be given to the Chinese and other comrades.

SOMETIMES I WISH I COULD READ!

The leaders of the Left Opposition pitted their politics against the Party apparatus. But they had no organisational trumps to play. Stalin held them all! In October 1927 Stalin assails the Opposition at a Politburo meeting. The Opposition is a Social-Democratic deviation! Admit your errors! Recant your views!

RECANT!

Ivan the Terrible, of Russia

Some months later, Trotsky delivers his last speech before the Central Committee, the leading body of the Communist Party. He is heard in silence. Even his opponents now realise they are witnessing the fall of a titan! Zinoviev does not even get a hearing. He is abused, heckled and insulted.

The First Secretary poses his candidature as the grave-digger of the Revolution!

The leaders of the Left Opposition, including Trotsky, are expelled from the Central Committee. Others are expelled from the Communist Party or arrested for circulating Oppositional literature.

7 November 1927: the Opposition attempts to appeal to the masses on the Tenth Anniversary the October Revolution. Stalinist strong-arm gangs break up the demonstrations. The masses watch silently. Their silence is decisive.

Zinoviev and Kamenev capitulate to Stalin in December 1927 and petition for re-admission to the Party as rank-and-file members.

Trotsky is alone—and decides to carry on fighting. Stalin wants to exile Trotsky 'legally' to Alma-Ata in remote Soviet Asia.

Trotsky is handed an order authorising his deportation in 1929:

"Under article 58/10 of the Criminal Code, on a charge of counter-revolutionary activity . . . Resolved: Citizen Trotsky to be deported from the territory of the USSR."

The decision of the GPU, criminal in substance and illegal in form, has been announced to me, 20 January 1929. **Trotsky.**

Trotsky will never see Russia again. He is bound for the Turkish island of Prinkipo. In the past, Prinkipo had been used by Byzantine Emperors to exile their opponents!

NO GOOD AT MEASURING FIELDS, BUT I'M SORRY TO SEE HIM GO!

Trotsky's expulsion was not the simple outcome of a duel between his personality and Stalin's. Rather, it was a radical struggle between Trotsky's principles of Permanent Revolution and Stalin's bureaucratic defense of "socialism in one country".

Trotsky's application for asylum is refused by the German SDP government. In Britain, the Labour Prime Minister Macdonald refuses though Lloyd George is in favour. H. G Wells, J. M. Keynes, Bernard Shaw and others appeal to the party to let Trotsky in.

Why does a Labour Government refuse the right of asylum to a distinguished socialist while granting it to reactionaries?

BECAUSE HE'S A **COMMIE** — THAT'S WHY!

Bernard Shaw

Winston Churchill

very European and North American state refuses him asylum. As these two continents own the other three, the planet is without a visa for Trotsky.

"But Trotsky cannot be silenced. His trenchant literary power and the hold, which his extraordinary career has given him on the public imagination of the modern world, enable him to use every attempt to persecute him. He becomes the inspirer and hero of all the militants of the extreme left of every country."
Bernard Shaw

 Outcast, stripped of political power, Trotsky is left with the weapon of his youth—his pen. And what a pen it will prove to be!
In exile Trotsky develops a Leninist analysis of world politics. From 1929 onwards he warns the Communist movement—and the world—about the growing crisis in Germany.

THE RISE OF HITLER

IN FOUR BLOODSTAINED ACTS

ACT 1

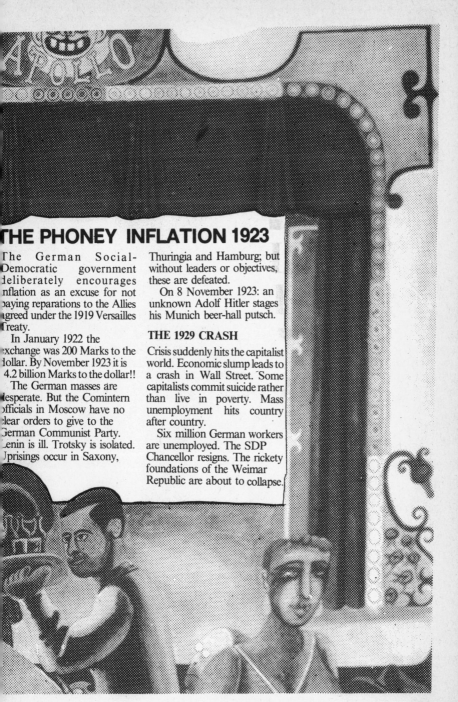

THE PHONEY INFLATION 1923

The German Social-Democratic government deliberately encourages inflation as an excuse for not paying reparations to the Allies agreed under the 1919 Versailles Treaty.

In January 1922 the exchange was 200 Marks to the dollar. By November 1923 it is 4.2 billion Marks to the dollar!!

The German masses are desperate. But the Comintern officials in Moscow have no clear orders to give to the German Communist Party. Lenin is ill. Trotsky is isolated. Uprisings occur in Saxony, Thuringia and Hamburg; but without leaders or objectives, these are defeated.

On 8 November 1923: an unknown Adolf Hitler stages his Munich beer-hall putsch.

THE 1929 CRASH

Crisis suddenly hits the capitalist world. Economic slump leads to a crash in Wall Street. Some capitalists commit suicide rather than live in poverty. Mass unemployment hits country after country.

Six million German workers are unemployed. The SDP Chancellor resigns. The rickety foundations of the Weimar Republic are about to collapse.

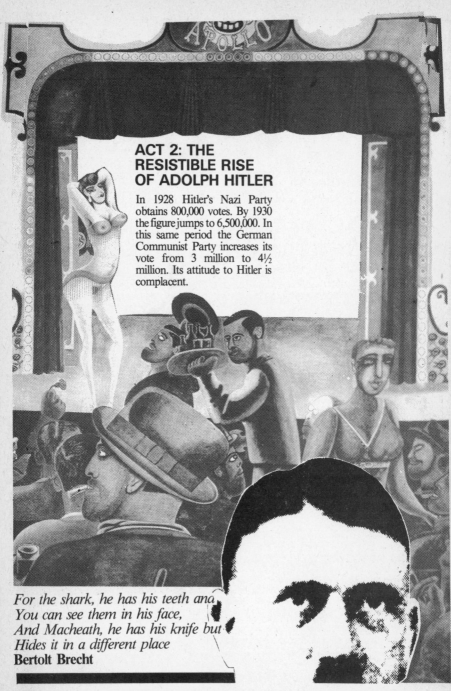

ACT 2: THE RESISTIBLE RISE OF ADOLPH HITLER

In 1928 Hitler's Nazi Party obtains 800,000 votes. By 1930 the figure jumps to 6,500,000. In this same period the German Communist Party increases its vote from 3 million to 4½ million. Its attitude to Hitler is complacent.

For the shark, he has his teeth and
You can see them in his face,
And Macheath, he has his knife but
Hides it in a different place
Bertolt Brecht

Ernst Thaelmann, Communist leader in the German Reichstag (parliament), sees no reason to panic over Hitler's 1930 sensational success.

"We stated soberly and seriously that 14 September 1930 was in a sense Hitler's best day after which there would be no better, but only worse days."
Thaelmann

Stalinist officials in the Comintern agree. Their orders to Thaelmann are, at all costs, to refuse a Communist-Socialist alliance. Social-Democrats are called social-fascists, and it is against them, not Hitler, that fire should be concentrated! Trotsky does not agree. For him, the Nazis are the party of counter-revolutionary despair; of the petit-bourgeois run amok.

Above: Thaelmann leads a Communist military band through Berlin.

Fascism raises to its feet those classes that are immediately above the proletariat and that are in dread of being forced down into its ranks; it organises and militarises them at the expense of finance capital, under the cover of the official government . . . Fascism is not merely a system of reprisals, of brutal force, and of police terror. Fascism is a particular governmental system based on the uprooting of all elements of proletarian democracy within bourgeois society.
Trotsky

Trotsky remains faithful to the United Front
strategy as accepted in 1922 by the Comintern. In
this spirit, he appeals to German Communists to
unite with Social-Democratic workers against Nazism.

*Worker-Communists, you are hundreds of thousands,
millions; you cannot leave for any place; there are not
enough passports for you. Should fascism come to
power, it will ride over your skulls and spines like a tank . .
. And only a fighting unity with Social Democratic
workers can bring victory. Make haste, you have very
little time left!*
Trotsky

Willie Munzenberg, a German Communist leader, replies:

Nothing could be as detrimental to the German working class and communism and nothing would promote fascism so much as the realisation of so criminal a proposal (Socialist - Communist unity)... He who proposes such a bloc only assists the social-fascists. His role is indeed ... plainly fascist.

This is the Comintern reply: to denounce Trotsky as a "social-fascist", a "fascist" and a "criminal". Trotsky ignores the abuse, shrugs off the slander and continues the struggle.

WHAT NOW, LITTLE MAN?

The German Communist Party continued to refuse a United Front with the socialist organisations. The result? Hitler comes to power in 1933.

In the concentration-camps and prisons of Hitler's Germany, the survivors of German social-democracy and communism will unite. It is the unity of the graveyard!

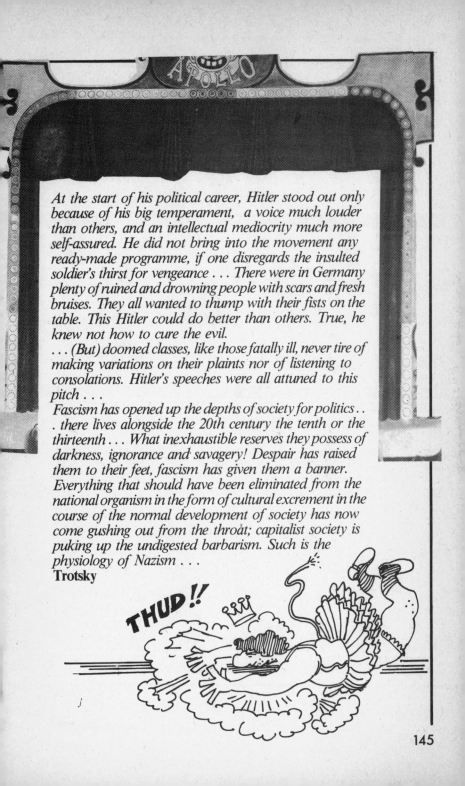

At the start of his political career, Hitler stood out only because of his big temperament, a voice much louder than others, and an intellectual mediocrity much more self-assured. He did not bring into the movement any ready-made programme, if one disregards the insulted soldier's thirst for vengeance . . . There were in Germany plenty of ruined and drowning people with scars and fresh bruises. They all wanted to thump with their fists on the table. This Hitler could do better than others. True, he knew not how to cure the evil.

. . . (But) doomed classes, like those fatally ill, never tire of making variations on their plaints nor of listening to consolations. Hitler's speeches were all attuned to this pitch . . .

Fascism has opened up the depths of society for politics . . . there lives alongside the 20th century the tenth or the thirteenth . . . What inexhaustible reserves they possess of darkness, ignorance and savagery! Despair has raised them to their feet, fascism has given them a banner. Everything that should have been eliminated from the national organism in the form of cultural excrement in the course of the normal development of society has now come gushing out from the throat; capitalist society is puking up the undigested barbarism. Such is the physiology of Nazism . . .

Trotsky

THUD!!

Was Hitler's victory inevitable? No. But the German Communist leaders were only partly to blame. The real authors of the mistake sit in Moscow at the head of the Comintern!

For Trotsky the debacle in Germany is truly the end of the road.
Stalinism cannot be reformed. It has become a cancer and has to be rooted out.

REVOLUTION BETRAYED

In 1936 Trotsky wrote his last major work, *The Revolution Betrayed*. In it he presents a complete, detailed criticism of Stalinism. It was the first attempt by a Marxist leader to grapple with the problems of the bureaucracy.

What is the bureaucracy?

For Trotsky it was a new ruling stratum, forming between 12 to 15% of the population. Material and political privileges rendered it conservative and counter-revolutionary. Its main concern is to preserve the status quo at home and abroad. It favours change only if necessary to preserve its powers.

What can be done about it?

It must be overthrown by force *from below*. In other words, a new revolution!

Yes, but a *political* one, to destroy the bureaucracy's power and privileges, to allow a plurality of Soviet parties and to restore the Soviets. The economic and social gains of the Revolution remain. The bureaucracy is not a new *class*, since its relations to the means of production are totally different. Nationalisation of the land, of the means of industrial production, transport and exchange, together with the monopoly of foreign trade, constitute the basis of Soviet social structure. Trotsky was to hold firm to this belief till his death.

147

ACT 3: STALIN PROCEEDS TO CONSTRUCT SOCIALISM IN ONE COUNTRY

Stalin announces the first Five-Year Plan in October 1928, a crash-program of industrialisation. To succeed, Stalin says the 'exploitative kulaks' must be eliminated as a class, and collectivisation of the farms begins. Stalin breaks with Bukharin and the Right Wing faction. It is their turn to be denounced as 'deviationists'!

Many millions perish of famine in 1932-33 because of Stalin's ruthless agrarian policy.

THE POPULAR FRONT

The 7th Congress of the Communist International meets in 1935. Its delegates are not aware that this is the last Comintern meeting. The Bulgarian leader Dimitrov places the burden of the German working class defeat on the shoulders of the German Communist Party.

The Popular Front is announced. It is conceived as an alliance between the Communist parties and the "democratic bourgeoisie" to defend democracy. Trotsky denounces it as –

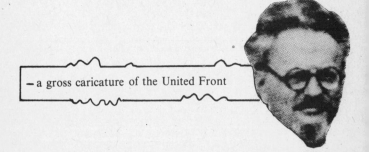

– a gross caricature of the United Front

We've had a foretaste of alliance with the "democratic bourgeoisie" in China 1927, remember? Precisely such an "alliance" had been rejected by Lenin in 1917 as Menshevik. But let's see where the Popular Front will lead . . .

FRANCE 1936

The strikes of May-June 1936 burst suddenly upon France with a new form of struggle unplanned by anyone — *the occupation of the factories!*

Leon Blum, a socialist, is in power with the Popular Front support of Communists and the bourgeois Radical Party. Blum promises social reforms, paid holidays and nationalisation of the war industries. The French Communist Party, under instruction from Moscow, ends the strikes and factory occupations.

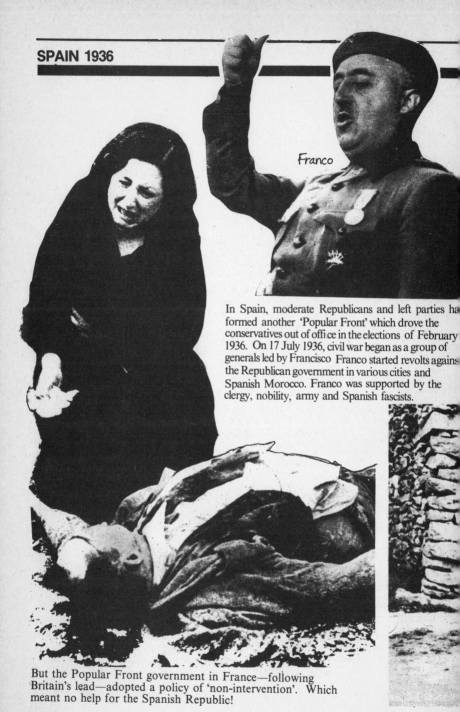

Franco

In Spain, moderate Republicans and left parties ha[ve] formed another 'Popular Front' which drove the conservatives out of office in the elections of February 1936. On 17 July 1936, civil war began as a group of generals led by Francisco Franco started revolts agains[t] the Republican government in various cities and Spanish Morocco. Franco was supported by the clergy, nobility, army and Spanish fascists.

But the Popular Front government in France—following Britain's lead—adopted a policy of 'non-intervention'. Which meant no help for the Spanish Republic!

Hitler and Mussolini didn't care a damn about non-intervention. They immediately sent arms and troops to help Franco. But the workers and peasants of the Spanish Republican armies, with some help from international volunteers, were still a match for Franco and his fascist cronies.

Stalin, after a few months of strict non-intervention, began sending help in 1936. Antonov-Ovseenko arrived as USSR Consul-General in Barcelona. Stalin's help will prove very costly!

Below: a Republican captured by fascist forces

Antonov-Ovseenko is recalled from Barcelona and executed in 1938. The tentacles of Stalin's purges now reach into Spain itself! While the war against Franco rages, Spanish supporters of Trotsky, anarchists and socialists are systematically imprisoned and murdered by Stalin's GPU agents in Spain.

The anti-fascist resistance was useful—up to a point. But Stalin had no desire to see the Republic win. Demoralisation did its work, and Spain fell to Franco in the spring of 1939.

THE PURGES HAVE BEGUN!

Before Stalin intervenes in Spain, an important event occurs. In August 1936, Zinoviev, Kamenev and 14 other old Bolsheviks are put on trial and executed.

This is only the beginning of other trials, other executions of top Soviet officials, old Bolsheviks and oppositionists.

What's going on?

The outcome of the first Five-Year Plan in 1933 had been a disaster. Stalin needed scapegoats.

In 1934 a Stalinist leader in Leningrad, Serge Kirov, was assassinated. Kirov had received more votes than Stalin at the preceding Party Congress. Kirov had also called for an end to the persecution of the oppositionists. Stalin had him killed. But the blame was put on Zinoviev and Kamenev, and the event was used to launch . . .

Kirov

THE GREATEST PURGE IN HISTORY

"To put to death the companions of Lenin, to decimate the old party, and to stand idly by while the working class of Spain was massacred, would have been to cast aside the mask, to offer the most serious food for Trotskyist criticism and to compromise even his remaining semblance of revolutionary prestige; while to appear before the Russian people and the working class of the world as the saviour of Spanish democracy, would compensate for plenty of misdeeds and politically consolidate his regime."
Victor Serge

ACT 4: DEMONISM AND INQUISITION

The purges, launched on an immense scale by Stalin in 1936, resemble the Catholic Inquisition. What was the Inquisition? Let King Philip II of Spain tell us . . .

Since all those outside the obedience and service of our Holy Mother the Catholic Church, fixed in their errors and heresies, strive to estrange pious and faithful Christians from our Holy Faith, we have decided that the true remedy is to avoid all contact with heretics and suspect persons and to extirpate their errors in order to avoid the danger of so great an offence to the Holy Faith and the Catholic Religion in this part of the world.

The General Apostolic Inquisitor of our realms and possessions, with the agreement of the members of the General Council of the Inquisition and after consulting Us, has decided to set up the Holy Office of the Inquisition in these new provinces.
Philip II 25 January 1569

nly change a few words—and the Stalinist inquisition is before you.

ictims of the Catholic Inquisition, exorcised of their demons through
rture, used to confess this way . . .

I am a satellite and disciple of Satan. For a long time I was a porter at the gate of hell, but several years ago, with eleven of my companions, I began to lay waste the kingdom of the Franks. As we were ordered, we destroyed the corn, the wine and all the other fruits produced by the earth for the use of man.

This sounds like the confessions of "Trotskyist-fascist-wreckers" accused of sabotaging Soviet industry and agriculture.
   Can you recognise Trotsky as Satan? Hard to believe? Just listen to Zinoviev at his trial . . .

' My defective Bolshevism became transformed into anti-Bolshevism, and through Trotskyism I arrived at Fascism. Trotskyism is a variety of fascism, and Zinovievism is a variety of Trotskyism... '

Stalin had promised that if Zinoviev and the others confessed their lives would be spared. They were all executed.

The old Bolshevik, Ivan Smirnov, "the Lenin of Siberia", was calm before his execution.

'We deserve this for our unworthy attitude at the trial'

SMIRNOV

Vozrozhdenye, a Tsarist exile newspaper, celebrated the first purge Trial of the Sixteen with a poem, 29 August 1936.

We thank thee, Stalin!
Sixteen scoundrels,
Sixteen butchers of the fatherland,
Have been gathered to their forefathers.

But why only Sixteen,
Give us Forty,
Give us hundreds,
Thousands,

Make a bridge across the Moscow river,
A bridge without towers and beams

A bridge of Soviet carrion
And add thy carcass
to the rest!

By the end of 1938 the Stalinist Terror had claimed 3 million victims—including Trotsky's first wife, Alexandra Sokolovskaya, who had remained an Oppositionist, and their two daughters. No one, at that time was yet aware of the extent of the killings. But Trotsky suspected that the trials were just the tip of an iceberg.

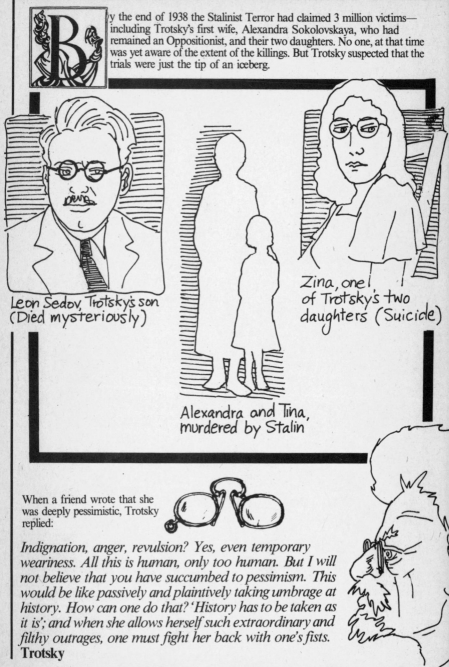

Leon Sedov, Trotsky's son (Died mysteriously)

Alexandra and Tina, murdered by Stalin

Zina, one of Trotsky's two daughters (Suicide)

When a friend wrote that she was deeply pessimistic, Trotsky replied:

Indignation, anger, revulsion? Yes, even temporary weariness. All this is human, only too human. But I will not believe that you have succumbed to pessimism. This would be like passively and plaintively taking umbrage at history. How can one do that? 'History has to be taken as it is'; and when she allows herself such extraordinary and filthy outrages, one must fight her back with one's fists.
Trotsky

160

Stalin destroyed every possible alternative to himself. The picture was bleak by 1939.

> *All anti-Stalinist forces had been wiped out; Trotskyism, Zinovievism and Bukharinism, all drowned in blood, had, like some Atlantis, vanished from all political horizons; and he himself, (Trotsky), was now the sole survivor of Atlantis.*
> **Isaac Deutscher**

Sole survivor? Not quite! Trotsky prepared for the founding conference of the Fourth International which took place in September 1938 in Paris. It was a gathering of Trotskyists from eleven countries. On the eve of the holocaust Trotsky re-affirms his belief in the ultimate destiny of the oppressed workers and peasants of the world. *Their right to rule!*

As Stalinism and Fascism traumatised the European working class, Trotsky remained the only Marxist theoretician who analysed both with dispassionate lucidity.
Exiled, Trotsky went from Turkey to France, Norway, and to Mexico where he spent the last three years of his life.

The flame of revolutionary passion burned in him as fierce and bright as ever. And he gave proof of a force of character superior to that which he had needed and had shown in 1917. **Isaac Deutscher**

The experiences of my life, in which there has been no lack of either success or failures, has not only not destroyed my faith in the clear, bright future of mankind, but, on the contrary, has given it an indestructible temper. This faith in reason, in truth, in human solidarity, which at the age of eighteen I took with me into the workers quarters of the provincial town of Nikolayev—this faith I have preserved more fully and completely. It has become more mature, but not less ardent. **Trotsky**

n 20 August 1940, a GPU agent, Ramon Mercader, assassinated Trotsky by a blow from an ice-pick to the skull. Trotsky died the next day and was buried in Mexico City.

TESTAMENT

For forty-three years of my conscious life I have remained a revolutionist; for forty-two of them I have fought under the banner of Marxism. If I had to begin all over again I would of course try to avoid this or that mistake, but the main course of my life would remain unchanged. I shall die a proletarian revolutionist, a Marxist, a dialectical materialist, and, consequently, an irreconcilable atheist. My faith in the communist future of mankind is not less ardent, indeed it is firmer today, than it was in the days of my youth. Natasha has just come up to the window from the courtyard and opened it wider so that the air may enter more freely into my room. I can see the bright green strip of grass beneath the wall, and the clear blue sky above the wall, and sunlight everywhere. Life is beautiful. Let the future generations cleanse it of all evil, oppression, and violence and enjoy it to the full.

Leon Trotsky
27 February 1940
Coyoacan, Mexico.

THE LEGACY OF TROTSKY

Trotsky's ideas, and his personality, continue to weave a spell on friends and enemies alike. What are the reasons for this?

He was the only one of Stalin's opponents who grasped what was happening in Russia and who, as a result of this knowledge, decided to fight. 'Stalinism is the syphilis of the labour movement.' Trotsky's struggle in exile was the only antibiotic which might have rid the international workers' movement of this disease. The fight to build new organisations was vital in order to preserve the legacy of Marx and Lenin. That fight is far from over.

Trotsky's legacy is the unfinished struggle: for proletarian democracy, for genuine socialism and the overcoming of bureaucracy, for social revolution in the 'Third World', for internationalism.

BOOKS ON TROTSKY

There are many, and steadily increasing numbers of books on aspects of Trotsky's life, his ideas and the 'puzzle' of his personality. The following are only a very few, intended to lead to more specialist reading, if that is wished.

Isaac Deutscher *The Prophet Armed, The Prophet Unarmed,* and *The Prophet Outcast,* Oxford University Press, in various editions available in the US and UK. This trilogy, a monumental biography, is a classic and remains indispensable. By far the best treatment of Trotsky's life and thought by a Marxist historian. Should be read with his *Stalin,* also available from OUP.

Irving Howe, *Leon Trotsky,* Oxford University Press and Viking Press, New York. Not unsympathetic to Trotsky. But does not entirely succeed in identifying his contribution to Marxism.

Ernest Mandel, *Trotsky: A study in the Dynamic of His Thought,* New Left Books, London and Schocken Books, New York. Excellent overall introduction to Trotsky's ideas. Also contains a useful critical bibliography for further reading.

Ronald Segal, *Leon Trotsky,* Pantheon Books, New York and Hutchinson, London. Good study of the 'paradoxes' behind Trotsky's relation to power.

Victor Serge, his novels about the Revolution provide truthful, sympathetic testimony: *Conquered City,* available in paperback from Writers and Readers, London and *The Case of Comrade Tulayev,* Doubleday, New York and Penguin Books, London. His non-fiction includes, *Memoirs of a Revolutionary,* Oxford University Press, *Year One of the Russian Revolution,* Allen Lane, The Penguin Press, London, and *From Lenin to Stalin,* Monad Press, New York.

Edmund Wilson, *To The Finland Station,* Farrar, Straus & Giroux, New York and Macmillan, London. Includes a sympathetic introductory portrait of Trotsky, as well as of Lenin, within the European radical tradition.

Bertram D. Wolfe, *Three Who Made A Revolution,* Dell, New York and Penguin, London. Contains a study of Trotsky, plus Lenin and Stalin, in the formative years prior to the 1917 Revolution.

BOOKS BY TROTSKY

From 1923 to 1927 the State Publishing House in Moscow produced 13 volumes of Trotsky's Collected Works and 5 volumes of his writings on military subjects. Stalin stopped them.

No complete collection in English yet exists; but *Pathfinder Press* New York, publishes the nearest thing to one, *Writings of Leon Trotsky 1929-1940,* 12 volumes, 1972-78.

Trotsky's major works, listed below, available in the US and UK from Pathfinder Press are referred to solely by publication date, unless otherwise stated.

The Challenge of the Left Opposition, 1975.
The First Five Years of the Communist International (2 volumes), Monad Press, New York 1973.
History of the Russian Revolution, 1976 and Pluto Press, London, 1976.
In Defense of Marxism, 1973
Leon Trotsky Speaks, 1972.
Literature and Revolution, University of Michigan Press, 1960.
Military Writings, 1969.
My Life, 1970 and Penguin Books, London, 1975.
1905, Penguin Books, London, 1974.
On Britain, Monad Press, New York, 1973.
On France, Monad Press, 1968.
The Permanent Revolution, 1969.
Problems of the Chinese Revolution, University of Michigan Press, 1967.
Problems of Everyday Life, Monad Press, New York, 1973.
Results and Prospects, 1978.
The Revolution Betrayed, 1972.
The Spanish Revolution (1931-39), 1972.
Stalin, Stein & Day, New York, 1970.
The Stalin School of Falsification, 1972.
The Struggle against Fascism in Germany, 1971 and Pelican, London, 1975.
Terrorism and Communism, University of Michigan Press, 1961.
Their Morals and Ours, New Park, 1974.
Third International After Lenin, 1971.
The Transitional Program for Socialist Revolution, 1973.
Trotsky's Diary in Exile, Atheneum Publishers, New York, 1964.
Women and the Family, 1973.

WHO'S WHO

Organisations

The Bund: in 1897 the secret cells of the Jewish Social-Democrats of Russian Poland and Lithuania held a meeting at Vilna and organised the General Union of Jewish Workers, known as the Bund. Mainly composed of factory-workers and artisans, it was Russia's first Social-Democratic mass organisation. It was part of the Russian Social-Democratic Labour Party (RSDLP) until the Party's 2nd Congress in 1903 when it opposed Lenin's concept of a centralist party. When its demand for a federated structure in which the Bund would represent Jewish workers was rejected, it split.

Central Committee: the elected executive body of the Bolshevik Party (and later, at the 7th Congress, March 1918, the Russian Communist Party). It is elected by delegates, themselves duly elected, to the Party Congresses. In May 1917 the Central Committee consisted of Lenin, Zinoviev, Kamenev, Milyutin, Nogin, Sverdlov, Smilga, Stalin and Fedorov.

Comintern: see **Third International**.

G.P.U.: the initials stand for State Political Directorate, the Soviet political police. Under Stalin it became the most powerful section of the state apparatus between 1922-34. Previously, between 1917-22 it was known as the Cheka, and after 1934 under various initials NKVD, MVD and KGB.

THE INTERNATIONALS:

The First International: shortened name of the International Workingmen's Association inspired by Karl Marx in 1864. After the defeat of the Paris Commune in 1871 and the onset of reaction it dwindled and was wound up in 1876.

The Second International: organised in 1889 as the successor to the First. A loose association of national and revolutionary elements. The organising Congress of 1889 met in Paris under the inspiring influence of the German Social-Democratic parliamentary victory over Bismarck. The outbreak of war in 1914 saw its major sections violating the elementary principles of socialist internationalism and supporting their respective imperialist governments. It fell apart during the First World War, but was revived as a reformist counter-pole to Leninism in 1923. It still has an office and a Secretary.

The Third International: the Communist International: the *Comintern,* organised by Lenin and the Bolsheviks in 1919 to guide nascent, world-wide Communist parties, and as a revolutionary successor to the Second. During Lenin's lifetime its world congresses were held annually. In 1943 Stalin dissolved the Comintern to show goodwill to Churchill and Roosevelt. But its Cold War shadow, the Cominform, based on the major European parties, survived till 1956.

The Fourth International: founded by Leon Trotsky in 1938 as a revolutionary successor to Stalin's Comintern. Trotsky's hopes of it becoming a mass international movement were mistaken. Isolation and persecution led to frequent splits. The 11th World Congress was held in 1979. While remaining the only organised revolutionary current on an international scale, the FI has yet to win a mass party to its ranks. Its best-known leader today is Ernest Mandel.

Mezhrayontsy: literally the Petrograd Interdistrict (Mezhrayonnaya), a loose-knit group of anti-war socialists which included Trotsky, Joffe, Ryazanov, Lunacharsky, Pokrovsky and other future leaders of the October Revolution, who were neither Bolsheviks nor Mensheviks when the group formed in 1913.

Narodnik: from *narod*, the people, populism. A democratic movement which arose in mid-19th century Russia. Its founders, radical intellectuals like Nikolai Chernyshevsky, Pavel Lavrov, Mikhail Bakunin, looked upon the peasantry as a revolutionary class and on communal forms of peasant economy as the nucleus of a uniquely Russian kind of socialism. Narodniks hoped Russia would come to socialism without going through a capitalist phase of historic development. Some Narodniks pursued terrorist methods, others preferred propaganda; some, like Plekhanov, turned to Marxism. Populism re-emerged as the influential Social-Revolutionary Party in 1902.

Politburo: executive committee of - and elected by - the Central Committee of the Russian Communist Party. Its formal organisation dates from the 8th Congress 1919 as the ruling body of the Party and the Soviet state. Its authority gradually shifted to Stalin. The first Politburo of 1919 consisted of Lenin, Trotsky, Kamenev, Bukharin and Stalin.

Social-Democracy: the name was borrowed from French republican politics of the 1840s by the German socialist Ferdinand Lassalle. Lassalle's followers believed in achieving socialism through state reforms and cooperatives. Another current of German socialism, the Eisenacher, led by a Marxist, Wilhelm Liebknecht, were more militant. In 1875, at Gotha, these two currents united to form the Socialist Labor Party of Germany. Marx's **Critique of the Gotha Programme:** Democratic Marxism was defined by Engels and Karl Kautsky in the Erfurt Programme of 1891. The names of Marx and Engels, its size and success in parliament, gave the German SDP great prestige. It was the guardian of orthodox Marxism, the model of the social-democratic mass movement of the 1890s and the leading party of the Second International. In 1898 the first congress of Russian Social-Democratic organisations met at Minsk with 6 delegates from Russia and 3 from the Bund and founded the Russian Social-Democratic Labour Party (RSDLP) as the political instrument of the Russian working class. The RSDLP believed that a bourgeois revolution, which would transform the Tsarist state into a liberal, capitalist democracy, must precede socialism. After the split at the 1903 London Congress, Lenin led the Bolshevik faction of the RSDLP to a final abandonment of the bourgeois revolution idea. Today, after the debacle of the First World War, the October Revolution and the rise of Hitler, the political meaning of Social-Democracy remains a non-revolutionary, centrist, parliamentary and state-form road to socialism.

Soviet: Russian for *council* generally; but now usually designates the specific institution which mobilised the masses, seized power and became (at first actually, later nominally) the government of Russia.

United Front: internationalist strategy devised by the Bolsheviks to unite the working class against the common enemy. Unity designed to combine all workers' parties regardless of their political affiliations in joint struggle. One major condition on the use of this tactic is that revolutionary parties must at all times preserve their political independence. Differs from the **Popular Front:** a tactic devised by the Bulgarian Stalinist, Georgi Dimitrov, in 1935 to enable Communist parties to move away from ultra-left sectarianism which had led to Hitler's victory. Sought to unite workers' parties with bourgeois ones to safeguard bourgeois democracy. But failed to do so both in Spain and France in the 1930s. The Popular Front can be seen as a precursor of Euro-Communism.

Biographies

Nikolai Ivanovich Bukharin (1888-1938): parents, Moscow schoolteachers. Joined the Bolsheviks as a student organiser 1906. Co-opted to the Moscow Party in 1908 and repeatedly arrested in the following years. Spent some time abroad. Returned to Moscow via Japan to take part in the October Revolution. Considered one of the Bolsheviks' leading theorists. Elected to the Central Committee at the 6th Party Congress. Occupied key positions in the revolution, as Politburo member, Comintern Executive Committee member, and for three years co-leader with Stalin of the Communist Party. Initially on the extreme left of the Party. After Lenin's death, moved to the right and linked up with Stalin in 1926 when he was appointed President of the Comintern. Served four years as Stalin's ideologist and apologist. After utilising him against the Left Opposition, Stalin had him arrested and tried. Main defendant at the Third Moscow Trial, found guilty and sentenced to death. Lenin had described him as the 'favorite of the Party', but also as 'soft wax...on which any demagogue can inscribe whatever he likes.'

Leon Blum (1872-1950): French statesman and socialist. Secretary of the parliamentary group of the Socialist Party. In 1921, when the Party split, he led the minority group that refused to allow the Socialist Party to be affiliated with the Third International. Headed the 1936 Popular Front bloc of Communists, Socialists and Radical Socialists. First Socialist to become premier, 1938. Imprisoned during the Nazi Occupation.

Chiang Kaishek (1887-1975): first met the great republican, Sun Yatsen, while attending Military College in Tokyo. Led the

bourgeois nationalist Kuomintang (People's Party) of China during the 1925-27 revolution. Hailed as an ally by Stalin. Chiang's April 1927 coup in Shanghai led to the massacre of Chinese Communists and trade-unionists. Defeated in 1949 by Mao Tsetung's Red Army and fled to Taiwan where he established a base from which his son still rules.

Friedrich Ebert (1871-1925): first President of the Weimar Republic. Became active in the trade union movement while a saddler and rose rapidly in the Socialist Party. Labour secretary in Bremen, elected to Reichstag (parliament) in 1912, voted for the war budget at the outbreak of World War One. Leader of the Majority Socialists in 1916. Became head of the provisional government of the German Republic in 1919 when Kaiser Wilhelm II abdicated. Another Social-Democrat, **Philipp Scheidemann** (1865-1939), became Chancellor of the Republic; and a trade-unionist member of the Reichstag, **Gustav Noske** (1868-1946) volunteered to act as military bloodhound in his post as Minister of Defence. Noske was responsible for the killings of the Spartacist leaders Rosa Luxemburg and Karl Liebknecht. He was President of Hanover 1920-33.

Francisco Franco (1892-1975): Spanish general and dictator, born in El Ferrol, province of Galicia. From Tetuan in Spanish Morocco organised transport of foreign legionnaires and colonial troops to the mainland to launch a coup d'état against the elected Republican government of Spain. Although Franco had military aid from Hitler and Mussolini to win the Civil War, he stayed neutral during the Second World War. At Burgos, 1936, Franco was invested with the title of El Caudillo. The United Nations resolution to isolate Franco diplomatically was revoked in 1950. Franco was in good standing with the Western Powers, receiving over $42 million in credit from the Export-Import Bank by 1951.

Adolph Abramovich Joffe (1883-1927): from a wealthy Jewish merchant family of the Crimea. Radical student. Studied in Berlin where he became a member of the RSDLP. Expelled from Germany in 1907 as an "undesirable alien". Drifted to Vienna where he met Trotsky and helped him to publish the Viennese *Pravda*. Life-long friendship with Trotsky. Joffe donated his entire inheritance to the Party. Suffered from nervous ailments and was treated by Freud's follower, Alfred Adler. Joined the Bolsheviks with Trotsky and the Mezhrayontsy in 1917 and was put on the Central Committee. Lenin greatly prized his gifts as a diplomat. Trotsky stated that the Revolution "did much more than psychoanalysis to liberate Joffe from his complexes." As Soviet ambassador to Berlin he made the embassy a centre for revolutionary propaganda. Expelled and diplomatic relations suspended. Illness and despair led him to commit suicide in 1926: an act which gained political significance because of his famous letter to Trotsky. His funeral was the last public demonstration by Trotskyists in the USSR.

Lev Borisovich Kamenev (Rosenfeld) (1883-1936): Trotsky's brother-in-law. Born in Moscow; father, engineer. Became attracted to Marxism as a student in Tiflis. In Paris, 1902, met Lenin and became a close supporter and committed Bolshevik. Edited *Proletary*, the Party's central organ. Leader of the Bolshevik faction in the 1914 Duma (Russian parliament under the Tsar). In 1914, with other RSDLP deputies, opposed Russia's entry into the war, was tried for treason, convicted and exiled to Turkhansk. Elected to the Central Committee, April 1917. Kamenev, like Zinoviev, opposed the October insurrection. Deputy Chairman under Lenin in the Council of People's Commissars and the Council of Labour and Defence. Appointed by Lenin himself as Lenin's literary executor and editor of Lenin's *Collected Works*. First president of the Lenin Institute. In 1919, at the front as an extraordinary representative of the Council of Defence. Shot by Stalin's order as a self-confessed traitor in the purges of 1936.

Karl Kautsky (1854-1938) one of foremost leaders and Marxist theorists of German Social-Democracy and the Second International prior to the war. In 1917 helped found the Independent Social-Democratic Party (USPD). When over half its members split in 1920 and joined the German Communist Party, Kautsky led the remainder back to the Second International in 1923. Became a leading opponent of the October Revolution and the subject of fierce attacks by Lenin and Trotsky who had once considered themselves his pupils.

Alexander Fyodorovich Kerensky (1881-1970): born, like Lenin, in Simbirsk of petty obility. Law graduate, 1904, specialised in defending socialists. Member of the outlawed Social-Revolutionary Party. Elected a Trudovik, or Labour Party, member to the Fourth Duma in 1912. Vice-Chairman of the Petrograd Soviet, but accepted post as Minister of Justice in the bourgeois provisional government formed by Prince Lvov in March 1917. Became Minister of War, May 1917, and continued the offensive against Germany and Austro-Hungary. Became Prime Minister after reorganisation of the provisional government in July, 1917. He fled Petrograd, and left Russia, when the Bolsheviks seized power.

Alexandra Mikhailovna Kollontai (1872-1952): from a wealthy land-owning family: her father, a Tsarist general. Privately educated, to isolate her from possible revolutionary contamination. Sympathetic to Narodnik terrorism. Early marriage to escape parental control did not last long. Joined educational and cultural societies, all concerned with aid to revolutionaries. Studied economics abroad. Became a Social-Democrat and Marxist. Witnessed the Bloody Sunday massacre of 9 January 1905. Organised meetings for women workers. Socialist feminist, held that women workers should not be organised separately from the Party, but that a special bureau inside the Party should defend their interests. Attracted to Bolshevism, but between 1905-5 was a Menshevik. Commissar for Bureau for Work Among Women in 1917. Member of the Workers' Opposition from 1919-22. Stalin detached her from the Left Opposition by making her a diplomat. As ambassador to Sweden she delivered Stalin's ultimatum to the government which had been prepared to grant Trotsky a visa. She died peacefully in Moscow—the only figure from the opposition whom Stalin did not execute.

Nikolai N. Krestinsky (1883-1938): born in Mogilyov on the Dnieper, son of radical intellectuals. Law graduate from St Petersburg University 1907. Remained a barrister till 1917. Bolshevik since 1907. Stood as Bolshevik candidate to the Fourth Duma elections. Arrested with other deputies and deported in 1914 to the Urals. People's Commissar for Finance in 1918 and later Deputy Commissar for Foreign Affairs till 1935. Made his mark as a Soviet diplomat after being sent abroad for his Trotskyist sympathies. Repudiated the Opposition in 1928. Expelled from the Party in 1935 and

tried in the Bukharin-Rykov Third Moscow Trial in 1938. Sentenced and shot. Rehabilitated October 27, 1963, via a lengthy appreciation in *Izvestia*.

Nadezhda Konstantinovna Krupskaya (1869-1939): born in St Petersburg, father a court official with liberal sympathies. 1891-6 worked as a teacher giving evening classes to workers. Became an early Marxist. Met Lenin, became his legal wife to accompany him into Siberian exile. Bolshevik Party worker. Commissar for Adult Education. Wrote numerous works on education. After Lenin's death wanted to make his Testament public. Her proposal was defeated by 30 votes to 10 on the Central Committee. Sympathised with the Opposition, but under threats and intimidation she capitulated to Stalin and remained a silent, tormented witness to the liquidation of Lenin's closest collaborators.

Bela Kun (1886-1939): leader of the Hungarian Communist Party and head of the short-lived Hungarian Soviet Republic 1919. Became a Comintern functionary with ultra-leftist views, and later a rabid anti-Trotskyist. Executed during the purges of 1939, but partially rehabilitated in 1956.

Yuri Osipovich Martov (Tsederbaum) (1873-1923): grandson of prominent Jewish editor and publicist. Began a revolutionary career as a student at St. Petersburg, expelled and arrested several times. In Vilna in the 1890s played an important role in the formation of the Bund and the rising labour movement. With Lenin, a founder of the League of Struggle for the Emancipation of the Working Class, and together with Lenin arrested in St Petersburg, 1896, and sentenced to Siberia. Editor and co-founder of *Iskra* in 1900 with Lenin, Plekhanov, Axelrod, Vera Zasulich and Potresov. Menshevik leader after 1905-7, favoured development of orthodox Marxist Social-Democracy by legal means. Opposed the outbreak of war but also Lenin's call for revolutionary civil war. Returned to Russia May 1917. Supported a socialist coalition government and was against Soviet seizure of power. At the Congress of Soviets in October spoke against the Bolshevik assault on the Winter Palace, and later Lenin's dissolution of the Constituent Assembly. In 1921 with Lenin's permission left for Germany.

Pavel N. Milyukov (1859-1943): distinguished historian, publicist and liberal politician. In 1895 forbidden to teach at Moscow University because of his liberal views. Leader of the Constitutional Democratic Party (Cadets) and prominent member of all the Dumas. Minister of Foreign Affairs in the Provisional Government, resigned April 1917. One of the more capable of the liberal bourgeois opponents of Bolshevism.

Willi Münzenberg: (1889-1940): German Communist leader, Secretary of the International Socialist Youth League 1914-21 and then the Young Communist International. Later an important organizer and Communist deputy in the Reichstag till 1933. Broke with the Party in 1937 after the Moscow Trials. Found hanged in France in 1940 after an escape from an internment camp. His death is variously ascribed to the Gestapo and the NKVD.

Alexander Lazarevich Parvus (Helfand) (1868-1924): born in Minsk province, raised in Odessa. Successful career as journalist in German left-wing press and as intermediary between German and Russian Social-Democrats. Organised publication of *Iskra* in Leipzig. With Trotsky, a leader of the 1915 Petersburg Soviet. Escaped from Siberia. Became extremely rich in Turkey and Balkans between 1910-15 and acted as go-between with German Ministry of Foreign Affairs. Arranged with Germany the safe-conduct of Lenin and others to Russia. Helped finance the Bolsheviks; but his shady pro-German dealings alienated Lenin who refused him entry to Russia after the October Revolution.

George Valentinovich Plekhanov (1856-1918): born Tambov province of noble family. While a student of mining in St. Petersburg, joined Narodniks. In 1897 he led a Narodnik faction, Chorny Peredel (Black Partition), which opposed terrorist methods. He abandoned Narodnik peasant socialism and in exile, with P.B. Axelrod and Vera Zasulich, formed the Marxist Emancipation of Labour group in 1883 which laid the foundation of Russian Social-Democracy. As intellectual leader of the movement, 'The father of Russian Marxism' influenced a whole generation of militants, including Lenin. His many writings popularised Marxism in Russia. He espoused the doctrine of economic determination which established a close relation between dialectical materialism and the physical sciences. After 1903 he sided with Mensheviks. In 1914 he insisted on participation in the defence of Russia and opposed the Bolshevik tactic of defeatism. He continued to oppose the Bolsheviks after the 1917 revolution, but was isolated from the Mensheviks too because of his pro-war stand. He died in exile in Finland.

Karl Berngardovich Radek (Sobelsohn) (1885-1939?): born in Lvov, Poland, brought up by his schoolteacher mother. Became a Marxist and Polish Social-Democrat. Emigrated to Berlin, but returned to Warsaw for the 1905 revolution. Brilliant journalist, notorious at assemblies for his savage tongue and wit. Both member of Polish and German Social-Democratic Parties, an opponent of Rosa Luxemburg. Attended the Zimmerwald and Keinthal anti-war conferences. Was in the Bolshevik Foreign Bureau in Stockholm during the October Revolution; but accompanied Trotsky to Brest-Litovsk. Member of the Central Committee and executive committee of the Comintern. Sent on a number of missions by the Comintern to Germany. Strong supporter of Trotsky and the Left Opposition. His subsequent capitulation to Stalin did not save him. Tried in 1937, found guilty, and sentenced to 10 years imprisonment. The circumstances of his death are unknown.

Christian Georgievich Rakovsky (1873-1941): born in Kotel, Bulgaria, of wealthy parents and notable family prominent in the struggle for independence against Turkey. Involved in politics as a 14-year-old schoolboy, emigrated at 17 to Geneva where he came under Plekhanov's influence. Connected with Russia by marriage, travelled there, and was active in Roumania and Bulgaria. Met Trotsky in 1903 and became a life-long friend. Close to left-Menshevism but persuaded by Trotsky to join the Bolsheviks. In 1918 Chairman of the Ukrainian Soviet and later Soviet ambassador to London and Paris. Fought bureaucracy and Stalin in 1923 on the question of nationalities. Joined the Left Opposition in 1927. But in 1934, because he considered the USSR in mortal danger from Fascism, he rallied to the leadership by capitulating to Stalin. The exiled Trotsky was shattered by this decision. Rakovsky was framed, accused of being a German agent, and sentenced to imprisonment at the Third

Moscow Trial in 1938. He died in a concentration camp, probably in 1941.

Victor Serge (Kibalchich) (1890-1947): born in Belgium, his father an exiled Narodnik and mother of Polish gentry. A relative, Nikolai Ivanovich Kibalchich, a Narodnik theorist, was a chemist accused of manufacturing the bombs that blew up Tsar Alexander II in 1881. Serge's political activity began in the anarchist movement of pre-1914 France. His friends were guillotined for their part in terrorism. 1917 found him in Barcelona taking part in a doomed uprising with his syndicalist comrades. Arriving in Russia in 1919 joined the Comintern as editor, administrator and agent abroad. Joined the Left Opposition, was imprisoned and deported to Central Asia. Exiled from Russia before the purge trials began. Serge's testimony as a novelist, poet, historian and journalist reflects the experience of three generations of revolutionaries - and their annihilation.

Alexander Gavrilovich Shliapnikov (1885-1937): from a poor artisan family of Old Believers in Murom. Three years elementary schooling, he became a qualified fitter and turner, and worked as a docker. Became a militant in the pre-1905 strike wave by reading revolutionary pamphlets. As a militant trade union organiser was often beaten up and arrested. Became a Bolshevik in 1907. Emigrated in 1908 and worked in several European factories. Returned to Russia during the war and in 1915 was Chairman of the Russian Bureau of the Central Committee. Helped set up the Petrograd Soviet in 1917. Chairman of the Metalworkers' Union, Soviet executive and Commissar for Labour in the first Soviet government. Organised the first armed workers' Red Guard in the legendary Vyborg District. On the left-wing of the Party. Together with Kollontai in 1921 founded the Workers' Opposition. Sent abroad as a diplomat in 1924. Returned in 1926 and capitulated to Stalin. Expelled from the party as a 'degenerate' in 1933. Refused to collaborate in a show trial, imprisoned and shot in 1937. Partially rehabilitated by the Procurator's Office in 1956.

Ernst Thaelmann (1886-1944): leader of the German Communist Party after its Stalinisation. Ran for President against Hindenburg and Hitler in 1932. Between 1924-33 leader of the Communist Party's Reichstag fraction.

Arrested by the Nazis in 1933 and murdered in a concentration camp at the end of the war.

Mikhail N. Tukhachevsky (1893-1937): from a land-owning family, joined Cadet Corps and graduated from a top Military Academy in 1914. Fought as lieutenant in the First World War and taken prisoner by the Germans. Escaped and returned. Joined the Bolsheviks in April 1918 and helped Trotsky create the Red Army. One of the revolution's leading military strategists, a fiery orator. Led the military suppression of the Kronstadt mutiny. Fell foul of Stalin, was tried and shot in the army purge in 1937. Refused to condemn Trotsky. Stalin had his entire family killed, except for his daughter. Rehabilitated after 1956.

Vera Zasulich (1851-1919): became a Narodnik militant while a student. Shot and wounded the Governor of St Petersburg, General Tepov, in protest against his arbitrary order under which a Narodnik student Bogolyubov was flogged for failing to remove his hat in Trepov's presence. Her trial and acquittal by the jury caused a sensation and · was popularly supported. Zasulich, with Plekhanov and others, passed from the Chrony Peredel Narodnik faction to Marxism, and in exile in Geneva helped to found Russian Social-Democracy, co-edited *Iskra* and sided with Mensheviks after 1903.

Grigori Yevseyevich Zinoviev (Radomylsky) (1883-1936): Born in Elizavetgrad, family of dairy farmers. No formal education. Social-Democrat at 18 and helped organise the first economic strikes in south Russia in 1890. Fled abroad, Met Lenin in 1903 and became a staunch supporter. From 1907 permanent member of the Bolshevik Central Committee, Lenin's closest assistant and co-editor of all his publications. Returned to Russia with Lenin's group. In hiding with Lenin after the abortive July uprising 1917. Despite his, and Kamenev's, disagreements with Lenin over October, remained top Bolshevik organiser. Chairman of Petrograd Soviet, in charge of North-West Russia 1918-19, and head of Comintern in 1919. In 1923-4 helped Stalin to defeat Trotsky. In 1925 with Kamenev led the 'Leningrad Opposition' which tried to oust Stalin but was defeated by the Stalin-Bukharin alliance. After lost all his main posts. Perished in the first purge, the Moscow Trial of August 1936.

BEGINNERS FOR BEGINNERS

Series Editor	**Richard Appignanesi**

Titles published in this series:

MARX FOR BEGINNERS

LENIN FOR BEGINNERS

MAO FOR BEGINNERS

TROTSKY FOR BEGINNERS

EINSTEIN FOR BEGINNERS

FREUD FOR BEGINNERS

CUBA FOR BEGINNERS

NUCLEAR POWER FOR BEGINNERS

Forthcoming titles:

Jesus	Darwin	Economists	Capitalism
Feminism	Anarchism	Socialism	Psychiatry
	Ecology	Food	

If you would like any further information about our books, please contact:

WRITERS AND READERS PUBLISHING COOPERATIVE,
9-19 RUPERT STREET · LONDON W1V 7FS

Telephone: 01·437 8942

D   R